About the Author

Martin Cohen is editor of *The Philosopher*, and one of today's best-known authors introducing key issues in philosophy, social science and politics to a wider audience. His books (more than 250,000 copies sold) have helped revolutionise the way mainstream philosophy is discussed and written about, spawning a new generation of popular introductions to the subject. Refusing to accept traditional constraints on subject matter and style, he has been aptly dubbed by his Taiwanese publisher as the 'enfant terrible' of philosophy.

Other recent books include *Wittgenstein's Beetle* and *Other Classic Thought Experiments* (Blackwell, 2004), *No Holiday: 80 Places You Don't Want to Visit* (Disinformation Travel Guides) (2006), *Philosophical Tales* (Blackwell, 2008), and the UK edition of *Philosophy for Dummies* (Wiley, 2010).

Martin Cohen

Mind Games

31 Days To REDISCOVER Your Brain

WILEY-BLACKWELL

A John Wiley & Sons, Ltd., Publication

This edition first published 2010
© 2010 John Wiley & Sons Inc

Blackwell Publishing was acquired by John Wiley & Sons in February 2007. Blackwell's publishing program has been merged with Wiley's global Scientific, Technical, and Medical business to form Wiley-Blackwell.

Registered Office
John Wiley & Sons Ltd, The Atrium, Southern Gate, Chichester, West Sussex,
PO19 8SQ, United Kingdom

Editorial Offices
350 Main Street, Malden, MA 02148-5020, USA
9600 Garsington Road, Oxford, OX4 2DQ, UK
The Atrium, Southern Gate, Chichester, West Sussex, PO19 8SQ, UK

For details of our global editorial offices, for customer services, and for information about how to apply for permission to reuse the copyright material in this book please see our website at www.wiley.com/wiley-blackwell.

Library of Congress Cataloging-in-Publication Data

Cohen, Martin, 1964–
    Mind games : 31 days to rediscover your brain / Martin Cohen.
       p. cm.
    Includes bibliographical references and index.
    ISBN 978-1-4443-3709-9 (pbk. : alk. paper)   1. Consciousness.   2. Thought experiments.   I. Title.
    B105.C477C62 2010
    128′.2–dc22

                         2010016200

A catalogue record for this book is available from the British Library.

Set in 10/12.5 pt Galliard by Toppan Best-set Premedia Limited
Printed and bound in Singapore by Fabulous Printers Pte Ltd

02   2011

Contents

Forward!

This is a book about thinking. We're going to follow Descartes and do a bit of thinking about thinking. Do monkeys think? Do plants? Not like us anyway. They just appear to do so, even as they follow preprogrammed evolutionary strategies. A bit like computers in fact. But, unlike computers, they are 'undoubtedly' conscious of something. For if nowadays everyone agrees that the body, indeed the whole universe, is a machine, still no one is quite able to say that there isn't a ghost riding along in the centre of it.

Descartes wrote 'I think, therefore I am', or at least, many people think he wrote that. He said awareness of the brute fact of existing was the only he thing he could be sure of, and used this nugget not only to get himself up in the morning but to rediscover the world. You see, Descartes was onto something. And that thing is consciousness. Perhaps this is the central mystery of philosophy. Science can explain everything else, but the strange sense of self-awareness it can only dismiss as an illusion.

So this book is really a celebration of consciousness, that goes under a rather more appealing title of *Mind Games*. There are plenty of these here, yes, but not merely in the evergreen Sudoku sense of puzzles and conceptual trickery, or in the scientific sense of explorations of the way the brain works, and often does not work, or even of 'thought experiments' in the widest philosophical sense of imaginary scenarios proceeding through the appliance of logic to factual hypotheses.

These are all very well, but the mind is more than that. It can also deal with things that do not exist, that do not make sense, that cannot be explained. Some people even think it can project thoughts instantaneously across distances, cause departed souls to rematerialise, and, of course, pass messages directly to the Creator. Yet if *serious* philosophers have been loath to countenance such irrationality, that's no reason to pass up an opportunity for practising some alternative mind games here. For science, like philosophy should be open to all questions and answers, not just those that fit the narrow fashions of the times.

And if you try all of the 31 experiments here, and if you still, by the end of it, can't remember what month it is let alone anything more impressively mathematical, still can't move objects by simply concentrating upon them, nor yet even see through verbal flim-flam to the essential argumentative core – if you read this book and yet somehow still cannot do any of that, I can offer you at least one thing. And that is that by the end of the course it will have turned out that the way you think, and the way I think, are not quite as individual as 'I think, therefore I am' implies. Because the human mind is created and renewed at every moment collectively, and no one of us can rediscover our sense of self, let alone rediscover our brain, entirely alone.

Acknowledgements

The illustrations have been specially drawn for this book by the French artist, Judit, with characteristic attention to the 'philosophical spirit' of the text. I should like especially to thank both her and Wiley-Blackwell's indefatigable and scholarly editor, Jeff Dean, for their support, enthusiasm, insights and ideas!

How To Use This Book

This book invites the reader to be active and to participate in the exploration of the ideas and in the experiments themselves. There are 'answers' at the back, avoiding the need to carry out all the activities, but these are not 'real answers' they are merely ideas and reflections on the issue, reflections that will be of more value – or quite possibly of no value – after you have tried the 'Mind Game' for yourself.

Now I know plenty of people (especially professors) who find it annoying to have to pause to think, let alone to actually try things out for themselves. Why not just say what we know about the state of current knowledge and give some suitable references to peer-reviewed papers? Surely that would be more logical? But the reason for this active approach is that the 'inconveniency' (as a famous philosopher termed such things) is also the opportunity to rediscover your brain – something too few books, let alone professors allow. And then too, in using these kinds of activities as starting points for philosophical discussions, I've been amazed at just how often people never even turn to the established authorities on the matters, but prefer to find solutions for themselves.

Many books go only part read. But even if you read only little bits of this book, that's fine. Because philosophy is not a body of knowledge, but an activity, and *Mind Games* is an opportunity – and an invitation – to enjoy that.

Influencing the Reptile Mind

Words

Task

Spend all day trying to think for *yourself*

But already, we're off to a bad start! These words you are now reading, whose are they?

Whose is that voice in your head? Yours or mine?

When you hear someone speak, the words remain theirs – to be ignored or disagreed with as you choose. But somehow to read someone's thoughts is to allow them, however temporarily, to take over the language centres of your brain. For as long as you are caught up in what they say, the writer becomes your inner voice.

Does that mean that, for a moment, the writer becomes the reader?

*Or does it mean instead that, for a moment, the reader becomes the writer?**

---

* All the tasks are discussed, explained and – just occasionally! – 'solved' in the Debriefing section which makes up the second half of the book. In this case, see p. 71 for a fairly brief contextual note.

Mind Games: 31 Days To REDISCOVER Your Brain, Martin Cohen © 2010 John Wiley & Sons Inc

Identifying the Reptile

Task

Identify, and talk to, the reptile in your head

According to one French psychologist, G. Clotaire Rapaille, most of our decisions are not determined rationally at all, perhaps using philosophy or even economics, but are taken surreptitiously in the twilight zone of the brain. These are decisions taken by what he calls 'the reptile mind', operating in the background, without us even being aware of it.

Dr Rapaille slithered to this understanding while working as a child psychologist, dedicated to helping children who had trouble communicating and expressing themselves. He found that most of their problems could be better understood if it was assumed that our human minds develop in three stages.

The theory

The earliest stage, the 'reptile' one, is simply concerned with survival. This is the stage in which we have to learn to breathe, to move around a bit, to eat. After a while, all this becomes unconscious.

The stage after this, which Dr Rapaille calls the limbic stage, is when children develop emotions and conscious preferences. It is when bonding takes place, for example between the child and its mother, and they

Mind Games: 31 Days To REDISCOVER Your Brain, Martin Cohen © 2010 John Wiley & Sons Inc

develop affection for certain things – for home, for warmth and for apple pudding, say.

The third and final stage, the one so beloved of philosophers, seems to occur after the age of seven, and sees the development of the outer brain, or the cortex – the part that gets studied and measured extensively by neurologists and other important-sounding scientists. This is the part – the only part – that deals with words, with numbers, with concepts. *But we learn many words before this stage.*

Dr Rapaille observed, in some children, that certain words produced certain problems, and these problems were, he realised, not attributable to the rational mind normally in charge of handling words, but went back much further, to when the word was first learnt. The children's difficulties were evidence, he decided, that each and every word we learn has a special significance. The word 'mummy', for instance, often claimed as the first one that baby 'learns', applies to just one person, who has a certain appearance and does certain motherly things. It is not just Mummy's voice, or Mummy's face, or even Mummy's smell that baby remembers. The word itself is 'imprinted' in baby's mind along with all the associations the word may have acquired: warmth, safety, love.

And the same is true for other less obvious words, such as *coffee, car,* or even *cigarettes.* 'When you learn a word, whatever it is, *coffee, love,* or *mother,* there is always a first time', Rapaille once explained, in a newspaper interview, adding: 'There's a first time to learn everything. The first time you understand, you imprint the meaning of this word; you create a mental connection that you're going to keep using the rest of your life.'

Rapaille calls this a code, an unconscious code in the brain. Each word was introduced to us at some point, and when it was 'imprinted' on our minds, it was with various associations. Finding these associations reveals each word's internalised, secret meaning.

The practice

So now, let's test the theory: what are the codes, say, for *coffee,* for *cars* or even for *cigarettes?*

Jot down your associations before you turn the page to see how they compare to the reptilian Doctor's ...
(Remember that these are not adjectives describing the thing but other things you link with it)

Coffee reminds me of:

1. . . . .
2. . . . .
3. . . . .

The car reminds me of:

1. . . . .
2. . . . .
3. . . . .

Cigarettes remind me of:

1. . . . .
2. . . . .
3. . . . .

When you've done that, pause a moment to admire your responses, and then turn to the debriefing section to see the answers.

The Fallacy of the Lonely Fact

Task

Try testing someone's sense of randomness. Offer them a little bet

You will toss a coin, say 20 times, and if in that run it comes up tails four times in a row, you win. If not they do. Of course, as such a thing is very unlikely, the wager will be in your favour: If you win, they must give you, say, a five zloty note – whereas if you fail to produce the run of four, you will pay them just one zloty. Such an arrangement only reflects the unlikeliness of getting a run of four tails in only 20 throws.

Suspicious types may accept the challenge – but only if it is swapped around to being a run of four heads! Of course, we can accept their bad faith. Because there are no tricks here.

Young people may prefer the wager in more saucy versions like 'I'll take off my shirt but you must take off ALL your clothes!' or drunk Russian philosophers may want to play variations involving holding partially loaded revolvers to each other's head. Equally, if you don't find anyone prepared to gamble with you, you can bet against yourself. It's safer that way. (But still not enough, I think, if playing Russian Roulette.)

Mind Games: 31 Days To REDISCOVER Your Brain, Martin Cohen © 2010 John Wiley & Sons Inc

The Immortals

Science fiction writers have long battled with philosophers over ways of extracting people's thoughts from their heads while alive and preserving them either in other people or merely in machines. And now neuropsychologists have moved in on the scene to do the same. But we need not be too technical in all this. For there exists already, and has for certainly three thousand years, a very simple way to preserve at least the most important thoughts in someone's head. And that immortality machine is called a book.

The main drawback with it is – even once it is published – the book still needs to be read.

And who can we rely on to do that after we are gone?

Mind Games: 31 Days To REDISCOVER Your Brain, Martin Cohen © 2010 John Wiley & Sons Inc

My Three Favourite Animals

Task

Complete an innocuous-looking survey using the imagination in order to try to find out a bit about the way our subconscious mind works

On the face of it, you just have to choose your three favourite animals. But to make the most of the test, use pen and paper and write down a sentence or two explaining your reasons too.

My first favourite animal is . . . . because . . . .

My second favourite animal is . . . . because . . . .

My third favourite animal is . . . . because . . . .

That's it!

ENZO 2008

The Prison of the Self

Task

Attempt to escape …

Around the time that Descartes published his *Meditations* with its famous 'cogito' – 'I think, therefore I am' – historians say that a kind of 'mutation' was taking place in human nature itself. This was the shift away from the collective consciousness of the group, be it defined by race or tribe or class, to the lone consciousness of the individual. And with it came feelings of isolation, of pointlessness and alienation. In fact, the historians talk of 'an epidemic' of depression in Europe.

Oliver Cromwell, the Lord Protector of briefly Republican England; John Bunyan, the Puritan writer of *Pilgrim's Progress*, and John Donne the exquisitely depressing poet, were amongst its victims. Take J.D. for instance. Many of Donne's exceedlingly dismal poems were written after the death of his wife, in 1617, and are particularly eloquent of sorrow. And since, for this investigation, we need to depress ourselves here is one of them:

> **'Death Be Not Proud' by John Donne**
>   Death be not proud, though some have called thee
> Mighty and dreadfull, for, thou art not soe, …
> Thou art slave to Fate, Chance, kings, and desperate men,
> And dost with poyson, warre, and sicknesse dwell,
> And poppie, or charmes can make us sleepe as well. …

Depressed? Now all you need to find is the cure.

Mind Games: 31 Days To REDISCOVER Your Brain, Martin Cohen © 2010 John Wiley & Sons Inc

Day 7

Trappism

Task

Don't talk to anyone

Religious folk have their rituals, most of them harmless, and some of them appalling, but there is at least one of them that touches upon something quite fundamental in human nature.

And that is the idea of the 'retreat' in which one goes away to a quiet corner of the world, and undertakes to spend days, weeks even, separated from all the trappings of modern life, *retreating* instead to a simpler existence: a little time to sleep, a little bit of food, and a lot of silence.

As to the last, there are people, like the Trappist monks of the Catholic tradition, who have dedicated their whole life to not talking. Are they mad? Or did they just become so. Because solitude has a habit of creeping up on you and playing tricks with the mind.

It is not actually necessary to become a monk to share the experience. Most people can adapt this experiment to their weekly routine. Simply decide not to talk to anyone for the weekend, far less, of course, listen to any machines. If you live near any empty hillsides, go out for long walks – on your own. Or, if you live in a sprawling city, spend the first day browsing in a bookshop (naturally, don't buy anything) and the second day pacing the back-ways.

It sounds easy enough not to talk, but try it and see.

Mind Games: 31 Days To REDISCOVER Your Brain, Martin Cohen © 2010 John Wiley & Sons Inc

Observing the Development of Little Minds

Week 2

Dotty Experiments on Teddies

> ## Task
>
> Get Piaget and Teddy to try to
> unconserve the numbers

Do children perceive the world quite differently from adults? In particular, could it be that they are completely illogical and *really* think magical things can happen which commonsense ought to tell them simply can't be the case?

A famous series of experiments by the French philosopher, Jean Piaget, seemed to prove what everyone had always suspected and that is that children really do inhabit a parallel universe.

One of these magical instances is how things can be made to appear and disappear. Piaget's demonstration was perhaps less interesting than others involving rabbits and top-hats but it is easier for us to replicate.

Simply put two rows of different things (say toffees and chocolate sweeties) on the table thus:

---

then ask the young child (Piaget thinks they should be under seven years old) whether there are more of one sort of object than of the other. The expected answer at this stage is 'Don't be silly, why of course there are the same number of both. Goodness, I would have thought that was obvious!'

But then rearrange the sweeties, and ask again, and Piaget claims a strange and ridiculous thing happens.

Now how many of each are there?

Another dotty experiment

Of course, you may have 'cheated' by counting the sweeties. But babies can't count. You know, very young babies, the kind that cannot obey simple instructions like 'stop crying' or 'don't throw that'. Because they have not learnt to speak yet, let alone listen. And so, it might seem obvious that these babies do not have any 'numbers' to count with – but then, neither do certain tribes with simpler languages than our own.

For instance, the Yupno people of highland Papua New Guinea are thought to have no specific number-words, yet still have a 'sense of number' as they can be seen to count (as young children like to do) using their body-parts, such as their fingers, toes and other bits too.

Anyway, we can test out baby's arithmetical abilities by putting two identical objects, perhaps teddies, behind a large piece of card, and then alternately secretly spiriting away or adding in an extra teddy. Every time we do this we should lift the card aside and exclaim to baby: 'Look!' And baby will (if we are lucky) look and see just one teddy! Or three!

When playing the trick, judge baby's reaction. Is baby following all this with interest? Gurgle!

And it seems babies follow all this number play with great interest, at least under experimental conditions. If our baby does, we can say, and researchers do say this, that it has already got a sense of 'number', trumping those who say that their baby is good at music or art or whatever, and indeed contrary to those philosophers and psychologists who consider that this number sense is so abstract that it only emerges much later in a child's development.

(a.m.)

The Cow in the Field-that-gets-built-on

Another game for children is called 'cows on the farm' and involves a piece of green cardboard, a small model cow and some wooden blocks. Actually, it is not much of a game, more like a mathematical exercise for testing children on their notions of area. Piaget flourished it when he wanted children to think they were going to play at being farmers when really they were about to do some geometry.

Anyway, with the children's agreement, however gained, a green farm was established. Not, that is to say, an organic one, merely a very green one. A little wooden cow was placed somewhere in the middle of its one field.

The first question is: will it make any difference to the amount of grass the cow has to feed on, whether it is placed in the middle of the field, or at the side, or even in one corner?

Most children (except perhaps the naughty ones) will say 'No'. Wherever the cow is placed in the field, it will have the same amount of grass to eat. Reassuring really. But being a cold, calculating philosopher, not a parent, Piaget would then proceed to 'develop' the land, by adding numbers of equally sized little cubes of wood, which represented farm buildings, to the field. On one development plan for the cow's field, half a dozen new barns were arranged in two tidy rows; in an alternative scheme, the same ones were spread randomly all around the field.

Mind Games: 31 Days To REDISCOVER Your Brain, Martin Cohen © 2010 John Wiley & Sons Inc

The question for the cow is, *which plan will leave it most grass to feed on?*

Plan A ...

Or Plan B?

(p.m.)
The Mountains of Egocentricity

Task

Construct a device to measure egocentricity

To recreate a final example of Piaget's celebrated investigations into the development of mind, we need a child subject and a three-dimensional landscape, perhaps three mountains made of papier mâché, although it might be enough to simply use a pile of books or cushions. Then we need to place (say) Jemima the doll on one side of the mountains/cushions and Teddy on the other. The arrangement should be varied so that sometimes, from where Teddy is, the 'mountains' prevent him from seeing Jemima, and sometimes he can see her.

The mountainscape might look something like the picture at the start of this section (page 13).

As you are doing this, ask your child subject, 'Can Teddy see Jemima?'

Mind Games: 31 Days To REDISCOVER Your Brain, Martin Cohen © 2010 John Wiley & Sons Inc

(evening)

Behave Yourself!

Task

Apply behaviourist principles to those around you*

All parents, just like all teachers, are interested in 'behaviour'. They may even be interested in *behaviourism*. This is the excellently simple theory that children (and animals) respond directly to stimuli.

Hurt them when they do something, and they stop doing it. Reward them when they do something else, and they will repeat the 'behaviour'. It sounds a dodgy theory, and it is. *But on the other hand …*

The problem for many parents is they seem to lose control of their children around … age three months. By the time the infant is two years old, the problems of 'bad behaviour' can be obvious. Junior won't eat spinach, but throws it at Mummy using the baby spoon as a weapon. At bedtime, when Mum and Dad are exhausted, Junior wants to stay up and play. Or if not exactly 'play', shout. Or if not shout, cry. It seems that the only way to satisfy these children is to give them chocolates, let them watch late night TV and cuddle them in bed.

---

*   If you have children, or even better, if you don't but know someone who does, apply behaviourist principles to them for a week and see what effect they have on achieving desired changes in 'behaviour'. If you prefer, apply the principles to your colleagues at work, or your partner – or just about anyone really.

Mind Games: 31 Days To REDISCOVER Your Brain, Martin Cohen © 2010 John Wiley & Sons Inc

Or is it? Could it be that (ahem!) this slightly unfashionable theory had something in it after all? That perhaps the advice of 'Supernanny' (as seen on TV) that parents need to take control, to jettison notions of family democracy for notions of family dictatorship, is right?

A rethink is needed, because, as a sober-voiced narrator puts it on one parenting show in the US, in some homes, the 'little monsters' have taken over the house.

What to do?

The Dissonance of the $1 Volunteers

Task

Make the children (or employees, or partners) do some boring repetitive activities

Dissonance is the feeling of uncomfortable tension which comes from holding two conflicting thoughts in the mind at the same time.

In a classic Stanford University experiment (one of those rather dodgy psychology ones, from 1959) students were obliged to perform repetitive and dull tasks such as turning pegs in holes at certain times and taking spools on and off trays.

If you want to try it …

- The first half-hour involved putting 12 spools onto a tray, emptying the tray, refilling it with spools, using one hand only.
- Then the second half-hour was spent turning 48 square pegs mounted on a board by clockwise quarter-turns.
- At the end of the session, the students were debriefed and dismissed. Invariably, the students reported that they found the sessions, supposedly to do with 'measures of performance', dull, boring and repetitive.

However, later, some of the students were recalled individually and asked to help the experimenters with their dull research as (they explained) the research assistant in charge of supervising the tasks had been taken ill. Or

Mind Games: 31 Days To REDISCOVER Your Brain, Martin Cohen © 2010 John Wiley & Sons Inc

maybe had gone mad. Anyway, the experimenters explained that the assistant's role included talking to waiting volunteers and explaining that the tasks they had just completed were in fact quite interesting. As invariably the students believed the opposite, accepting the job created a certain amount of cognitive dissonance.

The experimenters offered to pay their temporary assistants, but the amount varied from student to student (although they did not know it); some received $1 per volunteer recruited per session, some received $20. Some of the students refused to take the job at any price, while some cheated by taking the cash but actually criticising the tasks. These cheats were of course thrown out of the research study.

The experiment was designed to find out which of the new 'research assistants' – the ones paid $1 or the overpaid $20 ones – made responsible as they were for encouraging participation, now thought the activities weren't so dull after all.

Investigating Memory

Task

Memory test: how many of these words can you remember?

apple
cushions
walk
table
dog
blanket
night
sheets
flowers
dreams
copper
teapot
chair
sleep
pillow
moon
hat
pyjamas
book

Having carefully read this list, now consider the following interesting story.

'In routing over my wardrobe the other day I discovered a curious and far from satisfactory circumstance, namely that I have left all my silk neck

Mind Games: 31 Days To REDISCOVER Your Brain, Martin Cohen © 2010 John Wiley & Sons Inc

handkerchiefs at home,' wrote Charles Lutwidge Dodgson (remember who he was and why he is famous?) to his sister Mary, in a letter dated 6 March 1851.

In due course, Dodgson, aka Lewis Carroll, also wrote a whole book of 'memory tricks' which he called *Memoria Technica* (1875) to help him memorise 'logarithms of primes up to 41'. No one else wants to be able to do this, but Lewis Carroll's method was not limited to mathematical numbers. He used it to recall the specific gravities of metals too! To remember gold's gravity (19.36), for instance, he made a rhyme: 'Would you have enough Gold for your rents? / Invest in the seven per cents.' The last four consonants (c, n, t and s in 'cents') of the couplet represent the digits 1, 9, 3 and 6 (but I've forgotten how). And to memorise the year of Columbus's discovery of America, Carroll produced a mnemonic: 'Columbus sailed the world around, / Until America was FOUND.' The last three consonants (f, n, d) represent the digits 4, 9 and 2 of the year 1492.

This is less than fascinating stuff, but readers of another of Carroll's books, the slightly more popular *Alice's Adventures in Wonderland*, might occasionally notice the important role memory plays in the book. In the opening chapter, for example, the heroine, while going down the rabbit hole, wonders if her family will remember to give her cat milk. Later on, finding a bottle on a glass table, Alice stops and wonders if the drink is safe, thinking of children getting into danger just because 'they would not remember the simple rules' taught by their friends. And (crucial example of the importance of memory) she forgets the key on the table that earlier on she had been unable to reach because of her shrunken size.

The whole strange experience makes her feel as if she has lost her own identity. So to reassure herself she goes through various memory tests ranging from what she did the day before, how she felt, to whether she could remember things she learnt in mathematics, geography and music lessons. As the story subtly points out, forgetting things causes not only inconveniences but can even risk individuals, like Alice, losing their personal identity.

Now you can now test your memory by writing all the words in the list out.

Jargon for Dummies

Donald Mitchell – coauthor of *The 2,000 Percent Squared Solution* (a strategic management professor and management consultant in Boston) – tells the world, via that peculiar public noticeboard of Amazon.com, about an insight that came to him while coaching children's sports teams:

> Management needs to become more like medicine where clinical tests run by practicing doctors provide most of the insight for improvement, rather [than] a philosophical debating society run by hypothetical thinkers.

Yet, notwithstanding this, working with people *is* a philosophical experience. And there are plenty of hypothetical thinkers around to advise. There are experts who say 'treat people as you like to be treated' (which is Kant's line); ones who say that 'people are capable of almost anything' (which is a little like Plato, at least in the *Meno*, where he shows that the slave boy knows trigonometry); and ones who say that 'a manager's role is diminishing in today's economy', which we may count as a tribute to the Scottish advocate of laissez-faire and philosopher of money, Adam Smith.

Now test all the theories in the laboratory of reality

Try managing some people, say, in your own family. Or failing that, in the local football team/theatre society/bridge club. Or, failing that, in a philosophical debating society run by those hypothetical thinkers …

Mind Games: 31 Days To REDISCOVER Your Brain, Martin Cohen © 2010 John Wiley & Sons Inc

Be Lucky!

Task

Find out how unlucky you are

Equipment needed: this book

The philosopher of 'luck' is Richard Wiseman, a psychologist at a former technical college in the UK (that's three pieces of bad luck already*) and author of a book on the subject called *The Luck Factor* which has become quite popular. But that's not luck exactly. Anyway, Wiseman does not seem to be downcast. Instead, he carries out experiments to discover whether part of being 'lucky' is simply the attitude taken towards life's events, good and bad, and not so much the events themselves.

In one experiment, Wiseman took two groups of people, who considered themselves either naturally 'very lucky' or, alas, 'very unlucky'. He asked everyone individually to look in a newspaper and tell him how many photographs there were in it. On average, he found, the unlucky people took about two minutes to count the photographs whereas the lucky people took just a matter of seconds. This remarkable result merits further investigation.

We can continue the research by doing a similar thing with this book. First of all, like Wiseman, we need to place people in their appropriate category by asking 'Do you consider yourself to be lucky – or unlucky?' (If anyone who refuses to be put in either group, simply put them in the lucky category and tell them in future not to be so self-effacing.)

Now get them (you can start by trying it yourself) to count how many pictures there are in this book.

---

*   A 'psychologist' not a philosopher, at a 'new' university, and living in the UK – a country that's physically in Europe but thinks it's in America.

Mind Games: 31 Days To REDISCOVER Your Brain, Martin Cohen © 2010 John Wiley & Sons Inc

This Is Not a Self-help Book

Task

Boil down a self-help book

Buy (or better, steal or borrow) a self-help book. Read it and then boil down its 80,000 words of advice into two or three paragraphs. Or lines, if you can. Or maybe even words …

Mind Games: 31 Days To REDISCOVER Your Brain, Martin Cohen © 2010 John Wiley & Sons Inc

Experiments in *Practical* Philosophy

Day 15

The Upside-down Goggles

Task

Make – and wear – some special goggles

That usually rather dry American philosopher, Daniel Dennett, once described a famous psychological experiment, not only devised by but also tried out by George Stratton at the end of the nineteenth century. In the experiment, people were fitted with goggles that turned their entire field of vision upside down. Those sufficiently fit can replicate the effect by walking around the room on their hands: indeed everything *appears* upside down. However, being on their hands prevents even the fittest continuing the test by performing simple everyday actions such as making a cup of tea, or reading a newspaper.

So the best way to participate in this interesting experiment is to acquire some goggles to make everything look upside down (instructions on how to make them follow) – and then try going about your everyday life for a few weeks wearing them.

And for most people, a curious thing happens …

They can now see the world is upside down!

First: Make the goggles*

Start by making a headband using a piece of card about 50 by 11 cm wide (the side of a typical cardboard box will do very nicely for this). Cut a long 'letterbox' slit in it about 10 cm by 2.5 cm wide. Make two holes at either end and fit a piece of elastic to finish the headband.

---

* With acknowledgements to 'Mighty Truck of Stuff' and numerous very exciting websites on the Internet.

Mind Games: 31 Days To REDISCOVER Your Brain, Martin Cohen © 2010 John Wiley & Sons Inc

Now you need two more pieces of card about 16 by 11 cm wide. One should be solid; at least 1.5 mm thick, and the other should be special 'mirror' card (which is unfortunately something you don't see everyday in the corner shop, but then this is an important experiment). Fix the two bits of card together with glue or a stapler. Make a space in the mirror for your nose to fit into. Now cut two 3 cm long slits in to the card either side of the nose 'hole'. These slits should be 11.5 cm from each other (see diagram.) The mirror card can now slide into the headband.

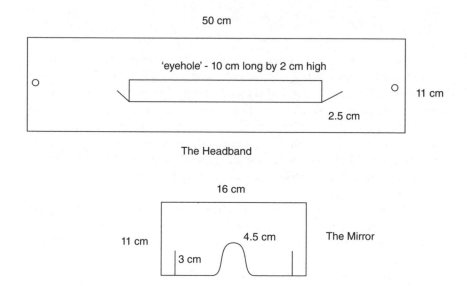

When you wear the headband, you should not be able to look directly ahead but should have to look through the eye-hole down on to the mirror cardboard.

Now do the test.

Fire-walking and Cold Baths

Task

Prepare a bed of red hot coals or wood embers

And that's not all! Next you have to walk on it.*
(Take care to wash your feet in cold water afterwards – in case there are bits of ember stuck between the toes.)
If you survive this without major burns, as many Indian fakirs and at least some 1960s hippies have done, you will gain an insight into the eternal struggle of 'mind over matter'.

Alternatively …

(Evening)

Task

Again, try to exert some control over your body

Some of us are just too cowardly to try out important explorations (like the fire-walking). At least we can all take a cold bath.

---

* Neither the author nor the publisher recommends or encourages walking on hot coals or wood embers, and anyone who undertakes such an activity does so solely at his or her own risk.

Mind Games: 31 Days To REDISCOVER Your Brain, Martin Cohen © 2010 John Wiley & Sons Inc

Run a cold bath.
Then add lots of bubble bath so that it looks hot.
Take your clothes off.
Get in the bath and have a long, leisurely soak saying to yourself 'Very relaxing! The water is just right.'

If you can make yourself believe that it is – does that constitute at least a small triumph of 'mind' over 'matter'?

Or just a triumph of mind over common sense?

R-pentomino

One of the few things about the world that seems clear, as well as fairly important, is the distinction between living and inanimate things. However, there is another kind of mathematical picture that blurs the distinction, that really does seem to be alive. It is a collection of dots on a grid which grow, separate, give birth and die, for all the mathematical world as if they were really microbes in a Petri dish.

These peculiar dotty pictures use no equations but simply follow a few rules. These rules are totally arbitrary, just as the fundamental constants guiding the universe seem to be arbitrary. Yet the instant the rules are varied the system loses that delicate balance between creation and extinction emblematic of 'life'. So the three rules that govern our dotty picture are not based on anything except the fact that they produce an intriguing result.

The three rules are:

Any dot which has either two or three neighbours (this is counting diagonals) survives to the next 'generation'.

Any dot that does not have two or three neighbours does not. It 'dies' and the square is empty in the next generation.

(Happily) any empty square which is touched by three, but not more and certainly not fewer, empty squares becomes a 'birth' square, with a new dot in it in the next generation.

The picture develops in discrete jumps or 'generations'. To start with, any number of dots can be randomly or aesthetically placed in squares on a grid. however we like. (Draughts on a chess board will do for small microbes.) Of course, the more dots there are, the more complicated. So for starters perhaps this one will do.

And here is what the molecule looks like after being left to 'react' for a couple of hundred 'generations'.

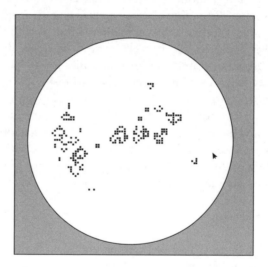

The mysterious life-form 'r-pentomino' (and friends) discovered in 1970 by mathematicians.

Now the question is, not so much 'How did it get here?' which is mathematics, but 'Is it alive?' which is philosophy.

(a.m.)

Proprioception (Scratching Noses Test)

Task

Fool your senses into believing your nose is several feet long

V.S. Ramchandran once devised some 'games' to illustrate how our perception of our own body can be easily confused. Some of them caused people to perceive other people's bodies as their own. In one such activity, one person – let's say, for literary reasons, Pinocchio – dons a blindfold, and sits behind someone else, both facing in the same direction. Then a third person takes Pinocchio's right hand and starts alternately tapping and stroking the nose of the person sitting in front of Pinocchio. So far, so predictable, but now the assistant takes Pinocchio's left hand and starts to alternately tap and stroke Pinocchio's own nose.

If it is done carefully, the blindfolded person begins to confuse the two sensations and imagines that they must belong to the same nose – one that, as for the wooden puppet Pinocchio in the tale, is now three feet long.

Mind Games: 31 Days To REDISCOVER Your Brain, Martin Cohen © 2010 John Wiley & Sons Inc

(p.m.)

Hear the McGurk Effect

Task

Fool your senses into hearing things that aren't there ...

Visual tricks are ten a penny. It is harder to play tricks on the ears. Yet it can be done.

For instance there is a curious phenomenon known as the McGurk Effect – a curious name in itself.

To reproduce the strange effect, we need a volunteer to listen, someone to mime, and someone to speak. The speaker only has to say one thing: BAA! BAA! BAAA!

Like a lost sheep, in fact. But they say this while standing immediately behind their assistant who mimes for them, That is, the assistant opens and shuts their mouth as though making a sound, but without making any (like pop stars do on supposedly 'live' TV shows). Meanwhile, the volunteer listener watches the lips of the person miming *without being able to see the lips of the person actually speaking*. You see how cunning it all is.

BA! BAA! BAAA! BA! BAA! BAAA!
goes the speaker. And the mimer mimes. But note – the trick is, their lips
  shape a different sound:
GA! GAA! GAAA! GA! GAA! GAAA!
Like a contented baby, perhaps. Whatever. Not the bleating sheep at all.
The listener watches their lips, in ignorance of course of the trick, and
  simply reports *what they have actually heard*.
And what will that be?

The best thing is to try it out for yourself.

Mind Games: 31 Days To REDISCOVER Your Brain, Martin Cohen © 2010 John Wiley & Sons Inc

Day 19

(a.m.)

Go for a Long Walk on the Much Too Long Coastal Path

Task

Measure it in centimetres

Coastal paths are often very scenic. But they can be dangerous. One of the least appreciated dangers is that they can be far longer than you realised and you get completely worn out.

Common sense tells us that a coastline has a certain length, as perhaps indicted in the atlas. Perhaps our walk is advertised as 10 kilometres. However, if we were to go on the walk with a measuring wheel of say, one metre in circumference, and wheel it carefully along the edge of the coast, taking in all the little irregularities, we would find it was a *lot* longer.

Worse still, if we were to throw away their one-metre wheel for a 10-centimetre one, we would now find even more irregularities that we had missed the first time. If we persistently scaled down and down to, say, the atomic level, we would still be finding irregularities that were adding to the total length. The problem becomes worse when you consider that the coastal path goes up and down too. This extra distance also needs to be added on.

The English scientist, Lewis Richardson, first worried about this inconsistency in the 1920s, noting that coastlines seem to have unmeasurable lengths and winds unmeasurable velocities.

Mind Games: 31 Days To REDISCOVER Your Brain, Martin Cohen © 2010 John Wiley & Sons Inc

For that reason, mathematicians like Richardson and Benoit Mandelbrot say that the length of a coastline is indeterminate – it essentially depends on the ruler you use to measure it.

Now the problem is – suppose we get lost (or simply give up) halfway along our much-longer-than-anticipated coastal walk? If our distance along it is arbitrary – *how can we telephone someone to come and pick us up?*

(p.m.)

Make a Bed of Nails

Task

Lie on it overnight*

(Take extra care when lying down and when getting up off the bed in the morning, and use a lump of wood as a pillow.)

Instructions for making the bed of nails (courtesy of Dave Wiley)

Materials required:

- Plywood board, 26″ × 56″ × 1″
- Panelling, 26″ × 56″ × 0.25″
- 12, 1″ flat-head wood screws
- 1375, 8″ aluminium gutter spikes

---

* Neither the author nor the publisher recommends or encourages lying on a bed of nails, and anyone who undertakes such an activity does so solely at his or her own risk.

Mind Games: 31 Days To REDISCOVER Your Brain, Martin Cohen © 2010 John Wiley & Sons Inc

Construction:

- Cut both boards to size.
- Mark a grid on the plywood with lines 1″ apart, parallel to the sides and ends.
- Drill a hole at each of the intersections, using a bit of the same diameter as the gutter spikes, or very slightly smaller, orthogonal to the board's surface.
- Drive a spike through each of the holes.
- Sandwich the nail heads between the plywood and the panelling, using the 1″ wood screws to secure the paneling to the plywood.
- If you wish to 'dress it up some', paint the boards after drilling the holes and use aluminium 'L' channelling to finish the edges.

Now Getting Really Rather Dangerous ...

Task

Look at something boring on the Internet

The Internet is full of boring websites, and has in many ways encouraged boring writing, boring 'blogging', boring 'interactive' games. (Hint: the 'microbes' of Day 17 are there, only they're NOT boring at all ...) But perhaps the most boring thing of them all is the idea of a little camera that takes pictures of something and automatically places it on the Internet every few minutes. Of course, this *could* be interesting too: there are the webcams in various dangerous places, such as on the edge of Mount St Helens volcano, which offers five-minute updates on the more-or-less continual eruptions there. Or there are the numerous 'sexy' webcams pioneered by an American student, Jennifer Ringley, in 1996 (when she was 19) which showed her doing everyday and arguably sexy things in her dormitory. At its peak, Jennicam recorded around three million 'hits' a day. Repeat: three million *a day*. That's more than the volcano did! Alas, it stopped in 2003 shortly after she started trying to charge surfers for the 'service'.

Another ethically suspect novelty was the website for the Texas Border Watch.

This, for 'one month only', was an experiment in which lots of webcams were connected up to provide live footage of the 1,240-mile-long Texas/Mexico frontier. The idea was to enlist the aid of the public in watching

Mind Games: 31 Days To REDISCOVER Your Brain, Martin Cohen © 2010 John Wiley & Sons Inc

the border and reporting any poor Mexicans they saw trying to sneak in to the land of welcome for huddled masses. Static images of wire-mesh fence stretching through arid scrubland proved irresistible viewing. In that one month, some 25 million people watched the webcams, and several thousand emails reporting incidents resulted. Texas now plans to open a full-time webcam public surveillance operation.

Now surf the net to find something boring ...

Doodle

Task

Draw something

Artists, like writers, like all creative types, know that the 'ideas' part is the hardest one. Not for nothing is Jackson Pollock-type random swirls of ink or paint derided – because it offends by trying to escape the planning stage. It seems very easy to produce pictures by splattering paper with different coloured paint, and entirely arbitrary to say which ones are more artistic – as essentially the results are random and unpredictable in advance. Yet, in a subtler way, 'representative art', of an Arcadian scene with the noble lord seated on his largest horse, is equally unimaginative, in as much as it follows reality. Splatter pictures and portraits, modern art and classical painting alike, are thus judged largely on technical criteria.

But we are not interested in all that. We just want to investigate the powers of someone's imagination. And for this a doodle will do.

Simply quickly sketch this: a simple picture containing a square, a circle and a cross somewhere in it.

Mind Games: 31 Days To REDISCOVER Your Brain, Martin Cohen © 2010 John Wiley & Sons Inc

Miscellaneous Philosophical Investigations

Week 4

(a.m.)
Molyneux's Problem

Task

No more dangerous tasks. Pause to
conceptualise

Part way through that treasure trove of Thought Experiments, John Locke's *Essay Concerning Human Understanding*, is a letter sent by 'a very ingenious and studious promoter of real knowledge', the scientist and politician, William Molyneux, to the great philosopher, posing a problem that invokes supposed differences between various kinds of perceptions.

Here is what Mr Molyneux says:

> Suppose a man born blind, and now adult, and taught by his touch to distinguish between a cube and a sphere of the same metal, and nighly [approximately] of the same bigness, so as to tell, when he felt one and the other, which is the cube, which the sphere. Suppose then the cube and sphere placed on a table, and the blind man be made to see: *quaere*, whether by his sight, before he touched them, he could now distinguish and tell which is the globe, which the cube?

Locke's 'acute and judicious' correspondent offers his own answer, which is briefly 'Not', explaining that though the visually challenged hypothetical

> has obtained the experience of how a globe, how a cube affects his touch, yet he has not yet obtained the experience, that what affects his touch so or so, must affect his sight so or so; or that a protuberant angle in the cube, that pressed his hand unequally, shall appear to his eye as it does in the cube.

But how would he know?

Mind Games: 31 Days To REDISCOVER Your Brain, Martin Cohen © 2010 John Wiley & Sons Inc

(p.m.)
Mary's Room

Task

Why is this one here?

A similar philosophical thought experiment to Mr Molly's old one, proposed by the Australian academic, Frank Jackson, in 1982, would be (like a rather dated black and white TV show) scarcely worth repeating were it not for the strange reactions of various eminent academic philosophers such as Daniel Dennett, David Lewis and Paul Churchland. (These were collected in a book called *There's Something About Mary*, in 2004.)

The thought experiment, as originally proposed, runs as follows:

> Mary is a brilliant scientist who is, for whatever reason, forced to investigate the world from a black and white room via a black and white television monitor. She specialises in the neurophysiology of vision and acquires, let us suppose, all the physical information there is to obtain about what goes on when we see ripe tomatoes, or the sky, and use terms like 'red', 'blue', and so on. She discovers, for example, just which wavelength combinations from the sky stimulate the retina, and exactly how this produces via the central nervous system the contraction of the vocal cords and expulsion of air from the lungs that results in the uttering of the sentence 'The sky is blue'.

Frank's challenge is: What will happen when Mary is released from her black and white room (or is given a colour television monitor)? Will she learn anything or not?

In other words, we are to imagine a scientist who knows everything there is to know about the science of colour, but has never experienced colour. Would Mary learn something new upon experiencing colour?

Mind Games: 31 Days To REDISCOVER Your Brain, Martin Cohen © 2010 John Wiley & Sons Inc

Unable To See Change

Task

Check who you are living or working with is the same person as yesterday

One time, as part of a cunning psychological investigation, some researchers stopped people on the street and asked them for directions. But in the middle of the passer-by explaining the way to the town hall, or wherever, two of the researchers' cronies would walk between the psychologists and their victim, carrying a door, temporarily obstructing their view of each other.

During this gap, another researcher would swap places with the first. Clad in a white coat and clutching a clip-board no doubt. The curious thing was that, in more than half of the cases, people continued to offer their advice to the researcher without spotting that the researcher had changed into someone else.

This raises the question:

How do we know that other people around us are not being changed too – our parents, people's children, even our friends?

Mind Games: 31 Days To REDISCOVER Your Brain, Martin Cohen © 2010 John Wiley & Sons Inc

Cascade Theory

Task

Chair (or rather rig) a discussion

Here's one you need a group for, the larger the better.

In the 1950s, the American social psychologist, Solomon Asch, found that people were quite prepared to change their minds on even quite straightforward factual matters, in order to 'go along with the crowd'.

In a famous experiment, he showed a group of volunteers cards with various lines drawn on them, and asked them to determine which of the lines were the longest. Unbeknown to one of the group, all the others were not, in fact, volunteers but stooges, previously instructed to assert things that really were obviously not the case, such as that a line that was obviously shorter than another was actually a bit longer ...

For example, see the image on page 143 as 'Appendix A'. ('Clues' have been added too.)

It turned out that, when enough of their companions told them to do so, around one third of people were all too prepared to change their minds, and (disregarding all the evidence) bend pliantly to peer pressure.

So, to do this experiment, prime your 'discussion' group to agree that, of the lines in Appendix A, B is longer but A and C are equal; the apparent mismatch being a well-known optical illusion. If you like, some of your stooges can apparently be 'led' to see this during the discussion!

You can develop the idea by ensuring that everyone is given three discussion starters of the kind that most of them will not be too sure what the correct answer is – if in fact there is one. For example:

Mind Games: 31 Days To REDISCOVER Your Brain, Martin Cohen © 2010 John Wiley & Sons Inc

- Low-fat diets reduce heart disease.
- Increased CO_2 emissions cause higher global temperatures.
- The series of *Harry Potter* books about a boy wizard is great fun for all ages, but especially children, and a jolly good read. It makes a very suitable present.

Or, if you can still remember it:

- The bestselling philosophy book *Sophie's World* is great fun for all ages, but especially children, *and* a jolly good introduction to philosophy.

Ask people to quietly write down their view to each on the paper on a scale of 1 to 5: 1 if they strongly agree, 5, if they disagree, 3 if they are neutral. (We can be a bit technical here.)

Then, say you want to reach a consensus on the issue by pooling everyone's information. Pick someone at random to start by saying what they think, and invite everyone else to feel free to change their ratings if they feel they are getting useful new information. Then work round the group, getting everyone's view.

However, the observation needed is not what 'the answer' is, but whether people are nudged towards a consensus.

Explain Yourself!

In life, someone leaves the house a minute late, bumps into an old friend who offers them a job as a secretary, is seen a year or two later in the office by a famous film director, becomes a film star – and is run over by a truck while on the way to Los Angeles to receive an Oscar. This is what mathematicians call 'sensitive dependence on initial conditions'. It is also, of course, what makes much in life largely unpredictable.

Most things in life vary in unpredictable ways, non-linear ways. Yet it is human nature to always look of patterns, scientist and investor alike. Yet the pattern may not be there.

Looking at the matter with 20/20 hindsight, should the person, acting as a 'rational agent', have refused the job offer to become a secretary – or only the opportunity to become a film star?

Mind Games: 31 Days To REDISCOVER Your Brain, Martin Cohen © 2010 John Wiley & Sons Inc

Investigating Un-Reason and Argument

A great way to always get your way is to play on the ambiguity of language. Since this is the source of most arguments too, it is also a tactic with some dangers. But suppose that we know perfectly well what someone means, but wish to misinterpret their words, then there are many ways to do this.

For example, suppose we are discussing Zeno's views of space and time, a suitably obscure subject.

> NAÏVE OPPONENT: You see, time is a continuum that cannot be divided up into instants – for otherwise the arrow would fall to the ground and Achilles would lose the race.
>
> YOU (*homing in on possible meanings of the word 'time'*): Do you mean that days cannot be divided up into hours and minutes?

(This confuses the issue as we are taking a conventional measure of time that by definition can be divided into other conventional measures of time.)

> NAÏVE OPPONENT: Days are by definition divided into hours and seconds. It does not matter what someone believes about time.

(Rats! Another card must be played – the ridiculous counter-example?)

> YOU: Well then, what about days? So you mean that days are nothing more than creations of convention – that the sun does not set at night – except by convention?

Who wins?

Mind Games: 31 Days To REDISCOVER Your Brain, Martin Cohen © 2010 John Wiley & Sons Inc

Subliminal Messages

Task

Become aware of hidden messages all around you

In the 1950s, the US economy was sluggish and enormous amounts of money were being spent on research into making people *want* to buy things. It was into this scene that a marketing expert called James Vicary stepped forward to announce to the usually equable Americans that he had just successfully persuaded a cinema audience to buy 20% more Coca Cola and a whopping 60% more popcorn during the intervals. All this simply by flashing 'Drink Coca-Cola' and 'Hungry? Eat Popcorn' frame messages during the film, which was, perhaps not irrelevantly, the movie *Picnic*, starring Kim Novak. Anyway, because the images lasted just 1/300 of a second, far too little for anyone to consciously be aware of them, it seemed both sneaky and effective ...

The experiment sparked off numerous efforts to identify subtle and not so subtle ways of influencing people's thoughts through the use of 'subliminal' messages. Radio stations played 'whispered messages' such as 'Buy Oklahoma Oil' while KTLA in Los Angeles persuaded (and is that not a triumph for the technique in itself?) the City to pay it $60000 dollars to Include subliminal public service messages in its broadcasts. Supermarkets installed cameras to watch customer eye movements (and found that many shoppers were in a sort of trance) and top TV shows started to contain apparently incidental shots of products or brands – for cars or drinks or lipstick – that were inserted, not for creative reasons but for 'green paper' ones, by the producers.

Mind Games: 31 Days To REDISCOVER Your Brain, Martin Cohen © 2010 John Wiley & Sons Inc

Similarly, lucrative self-help tapes ever since have to include subliminal messages such as 'I have high self-worth and high self-esteem' while others have taken to concealing messages for No particular purpose, other than that the message be 'hidden'. Pop groups, including the Beatles, hid various druggy messages in their covers and songs while the heavy metal rock group, Judas Priest, was taken to court for encouraging people to want to Kill themselves after it hid the Two-word message 'Do it' in a song. In the US Election of 2000, accusations were made by the Democrats that a Republican National Committee ad included subliminal messages intended to make people think of Al Gore as a rat.

Ever since, lots of people still do ... extraordinary!
Anyway, what's the hidden message in this piece?

Day 28

(a.m.)

The Power of Prayer

Task

Pray a little

Equipment needed: quiet, spiritual space, world leaders,* plane,* nuclear weapons*

This is a very simple philosophical, not to say theological, investigation.

To do this, we need only to think of something we would like to see changed, not to say 'improved', such as the weather, or maybe the progress of our favourite football team. Of course, it is important to be able to separate out changes due to our prayers from those that would have occurred anyway. For that reason, it may be better to

> pray that all the world leaders get killed in a plane crash on their way to a summit and nuclear Armageddon is triggered in the ensuing chaos.

Pray that this happens, on your hands and knees if you think it helps, say every evening for a week. (If the prayer seems rather negative, not to say unkind, for reasons that should become clear later, it is a 'safe' prayer to start with.)

Now, using conventional sensory methods, go outside each morning and see if it has happened.

---

*   Direct control of these elements is not required, merely that there be some somewhere.

Mind Games: 31 Days To REDISCOVER Your Brain, Martin Cohen © 2010 John Wiley & Sons Inc

(p.m.)
Pray for Good Crops

Equipment needed: seedlings, two plant pots, two watering cans

Here is a more modest test of the power of the mind to influence brute matter, involving those most fragile and sensitive elements of the plant kingdom – seedlings – and two jugs of water.

The element of mind comes in as one jug is infused with spiritual power by being prayed over, whilst the other jug is left just holding plain old water. If you like, you can also have a third pot of water which you curse regularly, to infuse it with 'negative vibrations'.

The experiment is simple: water one pot of seedlings with the 'holy' water, and one with the plain 'common or garden' water. If you have 'cursed' water, add a third pot of unfortunate seedlings. After a week or so, you should simply by measuring the plant growth – and all most scientifically – be able to demonstrate whether or not thoughts can be communicated to the sensitive seedlings in this evidently mysterious way.

Equipment to test the effects of holy water over cursed water.

Mind Games: 31 Days To REDISCOVER Your Brain, Martin Cohen © 2010 John Wiley & Sons Inc

The Horror and the Beauty
Or Vice Versa

Mind Games: 31 Days To REDISCOVER Your Brain, Martin Cohen © 2010 John Wiley & Sons Inc

Hildegard of Bingen, the tenth child of a family of German aristocrats way back in the twelfth century, counts amongst the somwhat depleted ranks of women writers as something of a philosopher. However, the source of her insights was not exactly philosophical: rather, starting in infancy, she experienced countless 'visions' of great clarity and beauty. One of the first of those was of one of the de Bingen cows giving birth to a calf. She saw the delicate animal very clearly: 'white ... marked with different coloured spots on its forehead, feet and back'. After this premonition came to pass, her astonished mother rewarded the little child with the new-born calf. Following further visions, at the age of eight, a greater reward followed, when her parents sent her off to the local convent for a life in holy orders.

Now most people have had visions, but we count them merely as dreams, and mostly the content is not much more remarkable than imagining, say, the colour of the spots on a piebald cow. And even if, in fact, such visions are part of a more profound metaphorical message, most of them will still be forgotten within a few minutes of waking.

Freud himself declared, in the dying years of the nineteenth century, that all dreams contain a 'psychical structure which has meaning' but, despite this backing, information obtained from 'the interpretation of dreams', let alone of 'visions', today has a dubious status. It doesn't help that Freud insisted that the true meaning of a dream was always sexual. (Hildegard herself was quick to interpret her dreams this way – mainly as warnings against the evil consequences of the sexual act, especially when undertaken purely for pleasure.)

However, Carl Jung, unlike his mentor, Freud, but like Hildegaard, considered dreams and visions to have much more power and deeper meanings than the merely physical or sensual.

And, at a key point in his life, when he was struggling to disconnect his life's work from Freudian psychology, he too had a vision, in his case a foreboding drama that seemed to predict a disaster.

In October, while I was alone on a journey, I was suddenly seized by an overpowering vision: I saw a monstrous flood covering all the northern and low-lying lands between the North Sea and the Alps. When it came up to Switzerland I saw that the mountains grew higher and higher to protect our country. I realised that a frightful catastrophe was in progress. I saw mighty yellow waves, the floating rubble of civilisation, and the drowned bodies of uncounted thousands. Then the whole sea turned to blood.

Two weeks passed; then the vision recurred, under the same conditions, even more vividly than before, with the blood even more emphasised. At the same time a voice spoke:

> Look at it well; it is wholly real and it will be so. You cannot doubt it.
> (Carl Jung, *Memories, Dreams and Reflections*, 1963)

So you can take your dreams more seriously and upgrade them to being 'visions'. Now they just need deciphering.

Strange Things

Task

Conduct some telepathy

Sir William F. Barrett, previously a respected physicist and scientist, once explained how he came to be one of the leading lights of the Society for Psychical Research (which until recently funded a Chair at the otherwise highly respectable Edinburgh University in Scotland). It seems it all started after he tried some experiments that led him to believe that something then new to science, which he provisionally called 'thought transference' and which later became known as 'telepathy', really existed.

At the first general meeting of the Society, on 17 July 1882, he read a paper entitled 'First Report on Mind Reading':

> There are several theories to explain the action of telepathy. The first compares it to wireless telegraphy. On this hypothesis it is supposed that it is due to ethereal wave action: Thought causes motion in the brain cells of the agent, the cells then impart motion to the surrounding ether in the form of waves which impinge on the brain cells of the percipient and give rise to a corresponding thought to that which started the ethereal wave motion.

This excellent theory would not be out of place in one of those pop science books by Stephen Pinker or Richard Dawkins – the kind full of stuff about 'neurons firing' in the brain and synapses opening and shutting like logic gates in an obedient computer. The only problem with it is that

Mind Games: 31 Days To REDISCOVER Your Brain, Martin Cohen © 2010 John Wiley & Sons Inc

it is obviously not the case. Fortunately, Sir William has plenty of other theories, only one of which need detain us here. And this is the idea that telepathy takes place in the subconscious mind, and that the subconscious mind of one person can be in touch with the minds of others 'by means of the universal mind underlying all things'. Individual subconscious minds are merely little bits of this 'universal mind'.

Actually, this is a little bit like the theory of Spinoza (the 'philosopher's philosopher') that each human mind is part of something eternal and indestructible. As he puts it in his very serious *Ethics*, the human mind 'cannot be absolutely destroyed with the body but something of it remains which is eternal'. Rubbish? Perhaps, But classy rubbish. Anyway, Spinoza has his own standard of proof:

> And though it is impossible that we should recollect that we existed before the body – since there cannot be any traces of this in the body, and eternity can neither be defined by time nor have any relation to time – still, we feel and know by Experience that we are eternal.

However, the Society for Psychical Research never decided which particular theory it preferred. And anyway, Sir William's interest is less in the theory than in the practice. He continues:

> My first experiment in the transmission of images of drawings and diagrams took place in the rooms of the Society for Psychical Research in May 1902. A private lady, Miss M. Telbin, acted as percipient, and I acted as agent. There were present at the time Mr J.G. Piddington, Honorary Secretary of the Society, and Mr Thomas, the then Acting Secretary.

All very proper, and quite above suspicion of any trickery.

> During the first experiment Miss Telbin, who was a stranger to me, sat with her back towards a large opaque screen. In front of her stood a small table upon which rested a crystal ball. She was asked to gaze – at the crystal and to describe any vision that might appear to form itself therein. (I may par-enthetically remark that the object of crystal-gazing is to concentrate the mind and to withdraw it from outward influences. The vision seen in the crystal does not exist objectively, but only in the mind of the seer.) On the other side of the screen, entirely hidden from the view of Miss Telbin, sat Mr Piddington and myself. This gentleman proceeded to take from a box which was behind the screen and on the floor between his and my chairs, various articles, and to hand them silently, one at a time, to me. I then concentrated my thoughts successively on each article. Miss Telbin gave an

account of what she saw in the crystal, and Mr Thomas, who sat in such a position that both Mr Piddington and myself were hidden from his view, took notes of what occurred.

The first article handed to Sir William was an engraving of Windsor Castle. He duly concentrated his thoughts on it, while Miss Telbin described the 'vision that presented itself to her mental view'.

Miss Telbin hazarded that she could see trees on the left side of the picture, and were those cottages on the left … ? and surely there was water – a moat perhaps? … but … alas … she mentioned no castle. This could have been discouraging. Even if, sometime later, during another experiment, Miss Telbin suddenly announced that a vision of Windsor Castle had just sprung into her mind!

This, Sir William noted soberly, must be regarded as a case of deferred telepathy.

What else could it be?

So now get a number of simple pictures – playing cards will do – and send the images telepathically to your friend sitting next door.

Manipulating Minds down on the Farm

Task

Read between the lines ...

When the famous left-wing author, George Orwell, died in 1950, the Head of the CIA, E. Howard Hunt (of later Watergate fame) immediately despatched his agents to 'England-near-London' to try to persuade Orwell's widow to sell them the film rights to *Animal Farm.*

This much-reprinted Socialist parable starts off when, one day, the animal workers of Manor Farm decide to throw out their lazy human owner and instead start dividing up the work (and the produce) of the farm fairly between them. They devise their own democracy with a mini-constitution of seven rules – painted on the side of the barn – that they all pledge to live by, such as: 'Whatever goes upon two legs is an enemy' and (most important): 'All animals are equal'.

But when, five years later, the film of *Animal Farm* came out, in a gloriously mad animated version, it was with a subtly different ending. In the last chapter of book, the farm animals sneak up to the window of the old farm and see inside the pigs and some neighbouring human farmers sitting around the kitchen table drinking and playing cards. However, in the final scene of the film, the image of the human neighbours gambling with the pigs is gone. Instead, now the animals peeking in the window see and reject only the nasty pigs.

And now the film's message is straightforward: Communism is bad.

Did that matter? It certainly simplified the plot ...

Mind Games: 31 Days To REDISCOVER Your Brain, Martin Cohen © 2010 John Wiley & Sons Inc

But worse was to come. Pleased with the response to *Animal Farm*, the CIA also obtained the film rights for *1984*, and guided by the same kind of respect for international law or the Geneva Conventions that they are famous for, immediately disregarded Orwell's specific instructions that his story could not be altered and tweaked its ending too. Recall that in *1984*, the book, Orwell describes a society in which, as Freud's nephew, Edward Bernays, had predicted all those years ago:

> Those who are in charge of controlling public opinion, are 'an invisible government', an elite who 'pull the wires that control the public mind'. (*Propaganda*, 1928)

By the end of the book, which starts with the clocks obediently striking 13, by command of the authorities, Orwell's hero, Winston Smith, after tentatively trying to 'resist', has been entirely defeated by the nightmarish all-seeing, all-knowing, all-controlling regime. The very last line says of him, bleakly, that now 'He loved Big Brother'.

Rewriting the end of *Animal Farm* is just one example of the often absurd lengths to which the CIA went in its crusade for capitalism and the American Way. With effectively unlimited money diverted from the reconstruction of Europe after the Second World War, channelled through organisations like the Farfield Foundation and the Congress for Cultural Freedom, it did much, much more. In fact, in the 50 years following the end of the Second World War, it remodelled the European intellectual mind.

- The CIA sponsored art exhibitions, intellectual conferences, concerts and magazines.
- It paid supporters to write features and opinion articles in newspapers.
- It funded publications of books, especially philosophy ones promoting 'the Enlightenment' and 'rationalism' ...
- It bankrolled some of the earliest exhibitions of Abstract Expressionist painting, such as Jackson Pollock's swirls of paint drops on a floor canvases.
- It translated and smuggled across the Iron Curtain strange works such as T.S. Eliot's *The Wasteland*.

All in a bid to undermine the cultural influence of Moscow. By the time the CIA had finished, no one knew who was an artistic or intellectual radical and who was a stooge and stool-pigeon.

But then, perhaps there *isn't* any difference?

Debriefing

Part II

Influencing the Reptile Mind

Week 1

Day 1

Words

The question is a tricky one, Paul Broks, a contemporary neurologist, or mind doctor as they might be called, raises this and many other strange issues in his book *Into the Silent Land*, and the phrase about 'the language centres of the brain' is his. Alas, he does not answer it. But then, it seems that neuroscience, like philosophy, has trouble dealing with the mysteries of consciousness. All Broks can tentatively offer is the insight that minds emerge from processes and interaction, and not from introspection as Descartes seemed to imagine. 'In a sense, we inhabit the space between things', says the Paul Broks. 'We subsist in emptiness.'

Day 2

Identifying the Reptile

Alas, when people are asked to answer questions like this, most of them try to use their 'intelligence'. After all, we all want to impress people. But naturally, intelligence is no use here. For the reptilian mind does not 'think'. It only remembers.

Mind Games: 31 Days To REDISCOVER Your Brain, Martin Cohen © 2010 John Wiley & Sons Inc

So throw away that first effort – product of the cerebral mind – and try again, and jot down now some of the other associations. And then, maybe, turn over that page too, and make a third list, this time putting down anything at all you happen to think of.

The 'answers'

Notice that (in English at least) each of our target words begins with 'c'. (Although he is French, Dr Rapaille works in America, using English.) Actually, I don't know if Dr Rapaille has proceeded much further than the third letter of the alphabet, but he scarcely need do so as he is already shockingly wealthy after applying his theory on behalf of another kind of entity that has trouble communicating – large corporations. In this way, he helped one particularly powerful, multinational food business to sell coffee to the Japanese – who up to then did not want any.

He also explained to another multinational how to sell more expensive, larger cars – even to customers who previously thought they wanted to be economical if not exactly ecological; and (most impressively of all) he helped a tobacco company to sell cigarettes to 'a new generation'.

How did he come to do it? What went wrong? Well, it seems it all started whilst he was still a doctor lecturing at Geneva University, and one of his students asked if his father could also come to hear his lecture. At the end of the lecture the father was very impressed and said to him, 'You know, doctor, I have a client for you.' And as Rapaille relates the story, he was flattered at this, and asked, 'Is it a little boy, little girl, that doesn't speak?' But the dad replied, 'No, no, it is Nestlé' (the huge Swiss chocky-food business). And of course Rapaille was very surprised, exclaiming: 'Nestlé? What can I do for Nestlé!' And then the man explained that the company were trying to sell instant coffee to the Japanese, and were not being very successful. Rapaille never looked back.

After all, as he explained later, therapeutic results with children are slow and hard to obtain. Marketing results with the general public are quick and easy. Not to mention, incredibly lucrative. All you need to know is 'the codes'.

So what are the codes? For the 3Cs, for example?

Coffee The key associations for many European coffee drinkers are 'aroma' and 'home'. Why? Because babies don't drink coffee – they don't like the taste. But they do remember the smell.

That's why coffee adverts always harp on about the aroma, and barely mention the taste. As Dr Rapaille explained to an American newspaper, adding:

I don't know if you remember this commercial, but it was really on code … You have a young guy coming from the Army in a uniform. Mother is upstairs asleep. He goes directly to the kitchen, 'Psssst,' open the coffee, and the smell – you know, because we designed the packaging to make sure that you smelled it right away.

… He prepares coffee; coffee goes up; the smell goes upstairs; the mother is asleep; she wakes up; she smiles. And we know the word she is going to say, because the code for aroma is 'home.' So she is going to say, 'Oh, he is home.' She rushed down the stairs, hugs the boy. I mean, we tested it. At P&G they test everything 400 times. People were crying. Why? Because we got the logic of emotion right.

The code for 'coffee' is childhood, home.

But not in Japan, on the other hand. Because the Japanese don't even have a childhood memory of coffee – what Rapaille calls the first imprint. What they have instead is a cultural fascination with tea. So the first thing Nestlé had to do was to give up trying to market coffee as an alternative to tea – and instead try to create a new group of customers ready 'imprinted' with a liking for coffee.

It did this by first marketing a dessert for children with a taste of coffee. Soon, it was able to start selling coffee through other things that were sweet, always playing surreptitiously on this childhood memory. 'And when the children were teenagers, the company found that they now had a big market for coffee in Japan,' finishes Rapaille proudly.

Cars And the car? What is the secret code for the car? Well, cars have two headlights and a grill; that is a face, and they have characters, that is, in a word, an identity. The purchasers like the car's 'identity' to match their image of themselves.

The code for car is 'look at me'.

On the other hand, if you ask people questions about their choice of car, they always answer with the 'cortex', so naturally they come up with good reasons: how fast it goes, how safe it is or how much petrol it uses. They don't realise that, in reality, they chose the car because they liked its 'face', its 'expression', its 'voice'.

If you ask them why they need, say, a four-wheel drive vehicle to go shopping, they will offer a lot of apparently rational explanations like: 'Well, you see, I need it because there might be a snowstorm' or "Well, you know, I sometimes go off-road' – explanations, however, which bear no relation to the person's real life.

Take that urban monster, the 'Hummer', a grotesquely inefficient car seemingly designed to run over pedestrians. The Hummer is typical of all the four-wheel drive, 'off-terrain' cars, with their kangaroo bars ready to crush children and animals that get in their way, The good doctor puts it this way: 'A car is a message. It has eyes, a mouth, a chin. It has a face, and that face speaks to you.' And the Hummer is 'a war machine' which says:

If you want to fight, I can fight. But you will die.

So why does anyone (apart from psychopaths – surely still a smaller market than non-psychopaths) want to buy such things? As Rapaille explains:

I think you need to go beyond words, and my training with autistic children is that I had to understand what these kids were trying to tell me with no words … How can I decode this kind of behaviour which is not a word? My theory is very simple: The reptilian always wins. I don't care what you're going to tell me intellectually. I don't care. Give me the reptilian. Why? Because the reptilian always wins.

Gun

Cigarettes And cigarettes? Rapaille found out that cigarettes are imprinted on children's minds as 'not allowed', as 'part of the adult world', and yes, as 'dangerous'.

The 'code' for cigarettes is forbidden, adult, risky.

Naturally then, when governments oblige tobacconists to put up notices saying their cigarettes are for sale only to adults, 'forbidden' to under-18s, and print on the boxes:

WARNING: Cigarettes kill!

they only *increase* the attractiveness of the product to the potential smoker.

Rituals

And then there is the 'ritual'. Cars, coffee, cigarettes – all can also be understood as rituals. Rapaille advised his tobacco-manufacturing clients to particularly emphasise the elements of ritual in their advertisements. Smoking and driving are rituals imprinted with a special power. They are initiation rites into adulthood.

Rituals serve specific functions:

- funeral rites serve to channel and control emotions
- birthdays and wedding anniversaries help to structure time
- rules of etiquette reinforce social bonds.

Rituals use certain techniques: repetition of elements. They have meanings that go beyond the immediate actions, they have mystical elements – chanting, special colours, movements, effects, fire; they are concerned with taboos, sometimes they are part of 'initiation ceremonies'.

Day 3

The Fallacy of the Lonely Fact

When it comes to runs of heads or tails, they are far more likely than we think. If you toss a coin 20 times, a run of four tails in a row (somewhere in the sequence) is no more unlikely than *not* getting four tails in a row. The odds of it happening are about evens. Yet, we seem to have an almost programmed-in tendency to see patterns in nature, even when there aren't any. It is part of the human quest for meaning and purpose, our way to structure a universe that may well just reflect the dance of energy, the play of randomness in the meaningless noise ...

Yes, yes, but a run of four tails! That seems very significant ... even when it isn't. If you can get anyone to accept your wager, you should make a tidy profit 'in the long run'. Indeed, in the short and medium run too. But, of course, anyone you ask to accept the wager can easily calculate the odds for themselves and see that. Well, maybe not *everyone*.

As the American stand-up comedia and social critic George Carlin once put it: 'Think about how stupid the average person is; now realise half of them are dumber than that.' Mind you, it depends on what George means by 'average'. For mathematicians, 'average' can mean either 'median', 'mean' – or mode.* So he's not so smart himself!

Sponge

---

* *An 11 year-old adds:* the 'median' is the middle value in a distribution, above and below which lie an equal number of values.

The 'mean' is a number that typifies a set of numbers, it could be a geometric mean or an arithmetic mean; this is often what people call the 'average'. The 'mode' is the value or item occurring most frequently in a series of observations or statistical data.

Sample data 1:
2, 5, 5, 6, 9, 12, 15

Here the 'mean' is 7.71, the 'median' is 6, and the 'mode' is 5

Sample data 2:
4, 5, 5, 5, 8, 12, 86

This time, the mean is 17.857, the median is 5, and the mode is also 5. George's 'average' is thus skewed heavily to one end of the range and no longer (er ...) 'means' what he meant.

The Immortals

Ah, but no one. That is why the French writer, Jean Dutourd, 'Grand officier de la Légion d'honneur', and author of a book, apparently intended to be funny, about a baby born with a dog's head (and some other doggy characteristics, like carrying a newspaper home in its mouth), once explained why he felt it was important to protect the language of Molière from contamination by the English. The English, that is, not so much in the guise of Shakespeare but in the form of those cartoon folks, the Simpsons.

Dutourd has a special responsibility, as he is a member of that peculiarly French institution of some 40 'intellectuals', l'Académie Française, (*élu en 1978 au fauteuil 31*) who, at least in theory, are charged with protecting the French language from unwelcome change. It is the Academy's job to make sure that in France, it is *courriels* that are sent, not emails, and that no one attempts to do *le shopping* at *le weekend* but instead continue to *faire les courses en fin de semaine*, even if it takes a bit longer.

For the Academy, it is an attempt to protect French history, French culture and French standards. But for Dutourd himself it is less complicated. As he told a French newspaper: 'I need a world that speaks French so that it can read my books. It's as simple as that.' Yet why should he care whether anyone continues to read his books, especially long after they have stopped buying them? However, it seems that Dutourd needs to be read in order to continue to feel important. More than that, indeed, in order to exist. For members of the Academy like to call themselves 'The Immortals', and *bien sur*, those whose thoughts live on forever in books achieve a kind of immortality.

So it is that Plato may not have had much success as an advisor to the King of Syracuse, but because all his books are still read, he has achieved a very enviable kind of immortality. But for himself, Dutourd is not so much an egotist as a deist – he considers his writings to have a direct effect on the universe: 'Each time I write a line, I modify the world', he says philosophically. Indeed, one time when unsure of how to finish a book, Dutourd asked God to complete it for him – which He promptly did.

Whether God really finished the book, or it was perhaps the 'collective consciousness', or just possibly even, Dutourd himself, is of no matter. The important thing is that nowadays, every time this book is picked up and read, the thought lives on – and so does the thinker. God, by finishing Dutourd's book, has assured His own immortality.

Ghost writers

Who *really* wrote the book?

Sometimes, quite ordinary people seem to come out with tales that seem much too, well, interesting for such quiet, well-behaved types. Shocking crime fiction tumbles from the pens of silver-haired ladies, racy sex-scenes from the typewriters of reliably dull politicians. Hidden depths? Ghost writers? Or two different minds within one body?

Robert Louis Stevenson, author of that profound psychological classic, *The Strange Case of Dr Jekyll and Mr Hyde*, said of the creative process that the ideas and the thoughts were not 'his' but were rather dictated to him by some mysterious other while he slept. At best, he was given the job of editing the ideas into book form. And what was more, this strange voice in his head lacked all the usual attributes of common decency, instead alternately shocking and fascinating him as he slept with its highly improper (but rather interesting) tales. Clearly, in fiction writing at least, the 'Dr Jekyll' part may be better at spelling, punctuation and grammar, but it is always to the appalling Mr Hyde that we return for the plot.

Day 5

My Three Favourite Animals

The choice of animals, alas, is totally irrelevant. However pleased we might be with our selection, it tells us nothing about ourselves and doubtless nothing about animals either. However, the reasons given for the choices are of much more interest. And of the three reasons, the third reason is the one that is by far the most interesting. Those who start off obediently but end up by messing about by the time of the third animal be warned! You may not so much be subverting the exercise as making it work …

This is because the first animal produces a response that matches your conventional values, your conventional view. Often the reason given for this animal is the thing we would like to be.

The second reason, on the other hand, is what we would like people to think about us. But by the time we are asked for a third reason many people inadvertently provide a surprising insight into themselves. The third reason reflects what we (subconsciously) believe people actually do say about ourselves. To all intents and purposes, this is the 'real us'.

So if someone says, for example, the they like cats best because they are cuddly, it means they would like to be cuddly themselves. If they say their second favourite animal is a dog because dogs are loyal, then that shows they would like people to think of them as loyal. But if they say (naively) for the third animal, that they like goldfish – because 'they sit about in a bowl all day not doing much', then they reveal that they recognise themselves as appearing to other people as 'sitting about all day not doing much'. And so this simple test brings us as near as we are ever likely to get to fulfilling the injunction of the Delphic Oracle: 'Know Thyself.'

The Prison of the Self

Some called it 'melancholy', the ancient term used by Hippocrates, others called it 'accide', the Latinate term preferred by the medieval church. The French sociologist Émile Durkheim called it 'anomie'. Nowadays it is simply called 'depression'. But the effects are the same. People become morose, lacking in energy, in a word – miserable. They also become sick, succumbing to diseases such as cancer or heart disease, or even commit suicide.

In 1733, one Dr George Cheyne counted such 'nervous disorders' as being responsible for almost one-third of the complaints of illness in England. He diagnosed the underlying cause as the miserable English weather, coupled with sedentary lifestyles and urbanisation. A flurry of books appeared offering remedies: one of the least famous was by one George Cheyne, who suggested a vegetarian diet.

Others, such as John Bunyan, wrote morally uplifting books, taking the line of Saint Augustine centuries earlier, and attributing the social sickness to pleasure in all its social guises – sexual relationships, banquets, festivals and celebrations – each one the devil's snare. For Bunyan, as for the Puritans generally, work was the proper cure for depression. Conflicting advice proffered by such as Robert Burton, an Anglican minister who-should-have-known-better, in *The Anatomy of Melancholy* in 1621, to take a little bit of time off, so that 'none shall be over-tired, but have their set times of recreations and holidays, to indulge their humour, feasts and merry meetings', the Puritans saw as dangerous quackery.

But who was right? Certainly cures need sound diagnoses to be effective. And was the root of the problem the dismantling of the elaborate social structures of collective entertainment – the fairs, the collective worship in churches – that had spread the virus of discontent? (In which case the kind of cure undertaken by Somali women might be appropriate – a musician is hired and everyone dances all day.) Or was it the dwindling number of opportunites for collective action – in defence of the community be it from internal enemies or (ideally) from 'outsiders'? For in wartime, perhaps rather surprisingly, suicide rates plummet. Or was it really the new over-emphasis on personal pleasure, coupled with disregard for God and Duty, as Bunyan thought?

Then again, could it have been, perhaps, something more simple, more mundane, that caused everyone to become depressed? Something like the invention of the mirror? These were just becoming part of every bourgeois household, along with that new sanctuary, the individual bedroom. Some big houses even had bathrooms and 'lavatories'! These were places in which the individual was free to 'be themselves' – whatever gloom that might bring.

Durkheim himself wrote (*Suicide*, 1897):

> Originally society is everything, the individual nothing ... But gradually things change. As societies become greater in volume and density, individual differences multiply, and the moment approaches when the only remaining bond among the members of a single human group will be just this: that they are all human.

Durkheim thought that it was rituals – especially religious ones – that served to break down the sense of isolation and reconnect sufferers with their community. They provided a release, however temporary, from the prison of the self.

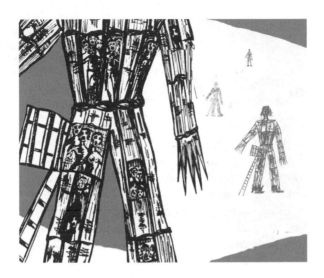

Very negativity

In 1882, the French Psychiatrist, Jules Cotard, described what he termed 'le délire de negation'. This is what happens when people have a very negative view of themselves. Such people not only worry that they may be ugly or stupid or unsuccessful, as most of us wonder from time to time, but believe that they have parts of their body either missing or rotting away, or even that they have become zombies – the living dead! Curiously, such thoughts are not exclusive to those suffering depression or other anxieties. Perfectly 'normal' people have suddenly become convinced that they have died – and sought medical advice on this, evidently rather awkward, personal health problem. But as to negativity, the cure is nothing a doctor can offer. The origin of the syndrome is thought to be buried deep in the part of the mind responsible for the most basic impulses, like hunger, pain and fear. So the best therapy may be simply activities that elicit similarly automatic (non-verbal) responses, but of a positive kind. An automatic response towards a baby or even a pet dog, to a tasty meal, to a beautiful view, may bypass the 'délire de negation'. On a good day …

Trappism

The human being is an animal that speaks and shouts and chats and laughs. Take that away, even briefly, and the world begins to change. Centuries of sophisticated social life slough off, leaving us lost and alone in the outer world and, what's worse, increasingly aware of the alternative inner one – of our thoughts.

Not for nothing do people mount a large television set in the corner of the room to talk to them all day, not for nothing do people attach little headphones to their heads when they must leave, however briefly, the range of the telly, the music or the radio. Because to see the world without the mental buzz of language is to recall an older and more terrifying existence.

In the glossy magazine of the French newspaper, *Le Figaro*, Philippe Dufay once described her 4,320 minutes of silence', as paying guest of the Trappist monks and nuns at the Benedictine Abbey of Jouarre.

Putting a few meagre possessions out in her 'cell', she started by studying a little book of poems written by an earlier Trappist monk, Christophe de Tibhirine, who found the deeper peace when he was assassinated in Algeria by Islamist rebels.

> Silence – that slow cure for misery.
> Silence – too great even for the solitude to contain.
> Silence that is an ocean of pain to harvest.
> Silence – the sign of a dear friend.

The Trappist day starts early, at about five o'clock in the morning, with chants in the church in the cold and dark. And then there is breakfast, but it is not a cheery affair, and is conducted, of course, in silence. The rest of the day is a sequence of prayers and chants. Nothing happens. Nothing but the essential: the chants, the readings, the duties. And hanging over the Abbey, the fields the ancient cloister, the weight of silence.

Attempting to emulate Christophe, Dufay writes of her own experiences in poetic style.

> Silences as heavy as lead, or silences as light as feathers, a rich feast of silences, succulent, worrying, nourishing, soothing or questioning.

It is inside the silent abbey, she adds, that we find, perhaps, the real world.

Day 8

Dotty Experiments on Teddies

Can babies count? Obviously, as everyone who has tried to swap three biscuits for two on the plate in front of a greedy infant knows, the answer is 'yes'. But psychologists have preferred to put things on a slightly more scientific basis. One of their favourite experiments (also, incidentally, providing young children with useful training for watching TV later on) measures the length of time babies stare at cards put immediately in front of their eyes.

The cards were not very interesting, consisting of just two or three large dots on a white background. For example, a card with two dots on it might be placed a few inches from the babies' eyes and the length of time they looked at it noted. Then another card with two dots on it, but spaced slightly further apart, might be placed in front of them – although this too was unlikely to produce little more than a quick glance. But contrast this with the reaction when the card was changed for one carrying three dots! Now the babies stare at the card fixedly, evidently struggling to work out something in their previously untroubled minds. Naturally, after a while they lose interest even in the three dots, but the researchers

Mind Games: 31 Days To REDISCOVER Your Brain, Martin Cohen © 2010 John Wiley & Sons Inc

found that they were then able to temporarily rekindle the interest by swapping the three-dots card with the two-dots one again.

Dots are all much of a muchness, but significantly, it seems, if three teddies are changed into two teddies and one doll, baby is markedly *less* interested than if they are changed into just two teddies. This sort of finding, in particular, has led psychologists to argue that babies have at least a rudimentary sense of number. One such, the ominous-sounding Dr Butterworth, claims that the experiments show not only that babies are aware that two and one make three, but that violations of arithmetic are more disturbing to them than changes of identity.

Sweeties and cows

Piaget found that the children nearly always replied that there were now more toffees than chocolates (and that there was less grass available for the cow under Plan B, as we'll see in a moment).

Through this, Piaget supposedly demonstrated that children lack the fundamental notion of the *conservation of number*, that is, the realisation that the number of things stays the same even if they are moved around and arranged differently.

This finding has had a great deal of influence in teaching circles, especially in the teaching of mathematics.

But there are general implications too. For thousand of years, artists painted children like miniature adults. They had baby-like bodies, but their heads were in the same proportion to the bodies as an adult's is to theirs. Only after the Renaissance did someone notice that in fact young children and especially babies are NOT the same as adults, and have proportionately much larger heads. Piaget's achievement was to convince people that maybe children do not think like rudimentary adults, but in a fundamentally different way.

This is surely true. However, Piaget himself may have underestimated the subtlety of children's thinking. Later researchers have found that if children do demonstrate the now-expected propensity to get the number of objects wrong, they also can unreliably get the number of sweeties right, thus thwarting Piaget's predictions. One researcher ingeniously repeated the sweeties experiment, but this time used a teddy bear to assist, so that when the researcher was apparently looking the other way, it was naughty teddy who rearranged the sweets!

Now when the researcher asked if the number of the sweeties was the same, the children were in no doubt, saying delightedly (having watched Teddy's activities with interest) 'No, they are exactly the same!'

(a.m.)

The Cow in the Field-that-gets built-on

Up until around the age of nine, children were sure that the cow in the first farm, the one with the neat line of buildings, had more grass and more grazing land available than the cow in the second farm in which the buildings had been spread about.

Of course, the children may have a more sophisticated idea of the consequences of building in the field than Piaget. If land around the buildings is also lost, or if the cow simply does not like grazing too near a building, it may make good practical sense in terms of 'grass available' for the houses to be grouped together.

Piaget's sweeties experiment concerned one-dimensional mathematical concepts, but the farm concerns the more sophisticated notions of 'area'. Indeed, Piaget also tested children's notions of 'volume' by pouring water from a jug first into a tall glass and then, refilling the jug, showing the children it was at the same level, and then pouring this into a flat dish.

He found that very young children were inclined to think that a tall, erect, narrow dish contained more liquid than an equal amount in a flat dish. Understanding that the volume must stay the same is said to require 'reverse thinking' and is the last of the Piagetian conservation tests children grasp.

Children, like animals, quickly develop some sense of numbers, but Piaget's point was that certain more abstract mathematical rules remain quite alien to them. Mathematical principles that philosophers like Aristotle and Descartes offered as so clear that they need not be doubted were, he showed, anything but clear to children.

The contemporary US researcher in the use of computers in education, Seymour Papert, inventor of a strange educational computer game called LOGO, once said that the 'core of Piaget' is his belief that looking carefully at how knowledge develops in children will tell us something about the philosophical nature of knowledge more generally too. Papert continued:

> In the past decade Piaget has been vigorously challenged by the current fashion of viewing knowledge as an intrinsic property of the brain. Ingenious

experiments have demonstrated that new-born infants already have some knowledge of the kind that Piaget saw as actively constructed by the growing child. But for those, like me, who still see Piaget as the giant in the field of cognitive theory, the difference between what the baby brings and what the adult has is so immense that the new discoveries do not significantly reduce the gap but only increase the mystery. (*Time* Magazine, special issue on 'The Century's Greatest Minds',29 March 1999, p. 105)

(p.m.)

The Mountains of Egocentricity

Curiously, Piaget found that young children would always report the answer as 'Yes'. As long as *they* could see Jemima, they assumed Teddy could. But what did that prove? Piaget thought it evidence that children cannot imagine the world from anyone's perspective except their own – they are, in a word, egocentric.

This explains why, as Piaget put it in his book on child psychology, *The Language and Thought of the Child* (1923), children sometimes speak as though talking aloud to themselves, even when, on the face of it, they are talking to someone else. Children often exhibit a calm indifference to the views or interests of their hearers, instead offering long monologues.

Piaget identified three kinds of 'egocentric' speech, which he arranged hierarchically in terms of supposed stages of social awareness.

STAGE ONE involves repetition of words and syllables serving no obvious social function.
STAGE TWO is where children talk to themselves, as if thinking aloud.
STAGE THREE is a new kind of monologues, 'collective monologues', in which a second person is needed to act as a stimulus for the child's speech but is not really expected to understand or even listen to it.

An expert adds:

Piaget viewed children as *little philosophers*, which he called *tiny thought-sacks* intent on building their own individual theories of knowledge. His theory could be enhanced by noting that *big philosophers* go through the three stages too, but in this case, the order is reversed. The less sophisticated philosopher still requires a second person to serve as a stimulus for their speech, even if they are not expected to understand it. At the second stage, the more mature philosopher speaks in long monologues during which they ruminate as if thinking aloud. And during the third and final stage, the most senior philosophers will repeat and invent combinations of words and syllables serving no obvious social function.

Anyway, returning to our little philosophers, Piaget considered ego-centric speech to be a necessary part of reflections and thought processes on the part of the child, intent on building models for understanding the world. However, he thought that as egocentric speech has no social func-tion, being a failure to communicate anything, so it must eventually fade away, disappearing as the child becomes more aware of the distinction between the inner and outer worlds.

He did not realise that big philosophers, on the other hand, celebrate their discipline's impracticality and apparent irrelevance to the daily world, value egocentricity and so can always see Jemima even when others can only see the mountains.

(evening)

Behave Yourself!

Supernanny's response is pure behaviourism:

Children will eat at fixed times, or they will not eat at all. They will eat what they are given; their 'tastes' do not enter into the question.
At bedtime, Mummy will not be available to lie down with Junior after all. Not at all. The child will go to bed at the fixed time and the light will go OFF.
For balance, there are rewards as well as with punishments. Those who eat their greens, go to bed on time, OBEY, will get word of praise too. But those who don't – remember! If they are naughty, there is always the 'naughty corner'.

The little girl in one family is accustomed to having Mum lie down next to her at bedtime. Forget it! says Supernanny, and the tradition is ended – without warning or explanation. When the girl screams, that only proves how *manipulative* she is. Later, Mum confesses, 'I felt like I was almost mistreating her.' 'Do not give in,' urges nanny, and sure enough, mis-givings soon yield to the report that 'it's working; it's getting quieter' – meaning that her daughter has abandoned hope that Mum will snuggle with her.

In the United Kingdom, at the turn of the millennium, the Labour government decided that indeed 'parenting skills' (or the lack of them) were the key to reforming society, and preventing what seems like a steady slide in public life and social standards. The origins of vandalism, random violence and general 'uncooperativeness' lay (the socialist government said) not with any failures of the state, but with a failure in the family home, much earlier on.

But not everyone would agree. Some 'alternative' households, run along hippy-lifestyle lines, seem to produce children who are creative, intelligent and considerate. Equally, a wealth of statistics show that 'bad behaviour' in societies seems to relate to the institutions and values of those societies as much as the values and practices of individual families. If, in a book or film, it is enough to understand the behaviour of a street thug by hearing the revelation that his Pa beat 'em (the whole family, little Sis 'n' all!) black and blue with a stick every night, there are plenty of 'problem' families where there was no Dad, no 'authority figure' and yet the children still 'went off the rails'. Simple explanations, like simple remedies, don't seem to fit the complex panoply of human behaviour.

Behaviourism

In his influential book, *Behaviourism* (1925) John Watson wrote:

> Give me a dozen healthy infants, well-formed, and my own specified world to bring them up in and I'll guarantee to take any one at random and train him to become any kind of specialist I might select – doctor, lawyer, artist, merchant-chief and yes, even beggar-man and thief, regardless of his talents, penchants, tendencies, abilities, vocations, and race of his ancestors.

Shortly after writing this, Watson left his position at an American university to work instead in business, to be precise, in the manipulative arts of marketing.

Day 10

The Dissonance of the $1 Volunteers

The study did not show that people change their beliefs given enough money – quite the opposite. The $1 students thought the activities were maybe not so bad – they had come to this conclusion as a way of 'justifying' their new role to themselves. By comparison, the $20 students had the crisp notes in their pockets to explain their actions, and continued to believe, frankly, that the sessions they were recommending were very, very dull.

Dissonance is a very powerful motivator that will often lead us to change one or other of the conflicting beliefs or actions. The discomfort often feels like a tension between the two opposing thoughts. It is most powerful when it is about our self-image, for example, if I believe I am good but find myself doing something bad. To release the tension we must either:

> *Change our behaviour ...*
> *or ...*
> *Change our beliefs.*

The experiment indicated that most people could 'convince themselves' that what they were doing was right. Ironically, the 'cheats', a handful, were those with stouter principles!

Investigating Memory

Most people can jot down a few. Don't feel too bad if after a few hours – or minutes even – you can't remember many; don't feel too bad if after a few weeks you can't remember *any*.

If you can do all of them, well, bully for you. If not, as many a boost-your-IQ book (and not just Lewis Carroll) will tell you, you can instead construct a story in which each of the worlds appears. 'The apple fell off the table and behind the cushions after the dog was taken for his walk ...' et cetera.

On the other hand, don't be too pleased if you can remember all of them. Oliver Sacks, the contemporary neurologist and writer, has described how certain kinds of brain damage result in enhanced memory, indeed the extraordinary ability apparently to recall, day by day, every event the individual has experienced. He surmises that the brain of the healthy individual contains a complete record of everything it has experienced since birth, but mercifully, most of this is inaccessible to our conscious mind.

But if you can't remember any, then it may be more serious. Because to the extent that you have lost your grip on the past, you may be unable to function in the present.

In *The Man Who Mistook his Wife for a Hat* (1985), a gripping account of the various kinds of disasters that can affect the brain, Oliver Sacks describes the case of one such memory-challenged person, Jimmie, 'the Lost Mariner', a man in his sixties whose memory has erased any recollections of events that occurred after his thirtieth year, and thus is continually shocked at the changes all around him, both in the physical world and, most horrifyingly, to the people he knows (if he recognises them). 'Guess some people age fast', he says, in an attempt at explanation.

Dr Sacks tries to substitute for the failure of Jimmie's memory by providing him with a simple backup system – a notepad. Jimmie writes down events in his diary and then can be asked to refer back to them. How well does that work? Yet not so well. For a start, such tricks serve to 'jog' memory. Jimmie simply does not recognise the entries as his own. 'Did I write that?' he asks, let alone 'Did I do that?' When asked how he is feeling, the answer is rather sad. He says: 'How do I feel? I cannot say I feel ill. But I cannot say I feel well. I cannot say I feel anything at all.' And he scratches his head in bewilderment. Sacks presses on though.

> 'Are you miserable?'
> 'Can't say that I am.'
> 'Do you enjoy life?'
> 'I can't say that I do ... '
> 'You don't enjoy life. How then do you *feel* about life?'

As to this Jimmie has the rather frank response: 'I can't say that I feel anything at all.' Dr Sacks protests, as a medical clinician must: 'You feel alive though?' but Jimmie, looking infinitely sad, says rather 'Feel alive? I haven't felt alive for a very long time.'

Curiously, in this limited way, Jimmie does have a sense of the lost years. Dr Sacks wonders what can be done to help someone apparently lost in a 'ten minute world' of fluctuating, transient events. He refers to a passage from his professional 'Bible', *The Neuropsychology of Memory*, by A.R. Luria: Herein, he reads:

> But a man does not consist of memory alone. He has feeling, will, sensibilities, moral being – matters on which neuropsychology cannot speak. And it is here, beyond the realm of an impersonal psychology, that you may find ways to touch him, and change him.

Indeed, whilst in chapel singing or praying, or whilst playing certain games or solving tricky puzzles, Jimmie does become a different, more complete person. For the instants that he is fully occupied with the present, his loss of the past ceases to trouble him. Yet Jimmie cannot spend all this time praying or solving puzzles ...

When Dr Sacks gives Jimmie the hospital garden to look after, Jimmie begins to make good progress. At first, every day the garden is 'new' to him, he has to 'rediscover it afresh each time', but after a while he begins to remember it, and is able to build upon his plans and strategies for tending it. As Sacks puts it, Jimmie is lost in space-time but located in 'intentional' time. He lives in 'a Kierkegaardian world'. Instead of things being organised in time and in space, they are organised by aesthetic, religious, moral and dramatic *feelings*.

The smell of coffee – again!

Dr Sacks also describes the case of a man who has had his sense of smell irretrievably destroyed. Smell is a subtle sense, which affects our everyday life far more than we realise. The interesting thing about the case, however, is not how much he suffered, far less how he came to terms with the loss, but that one day he found a drink brought to him yielded up that rich aroma of coffee again. The same miracle happened when he took out his pipe and filled it with tobacco.

But the medical facts remained unchanged. His nose could no more detect smells than his ears could. The scents he was savouring were entirely in his mind, yet not imagined, exactly. They were previous olfactory experiences being faithfully *replayed* at the correct moment by a helpful subconscious mind.

Confabulous!

Psychologists think that our memories work by constructing narratives, 'confabulating', that enable us to think of our past as a continuous and coherent string of events, even when the events do not really fit the pattern we impose. That is why those memory gurus advise those wishing to retain unrelated information to construct a story including each object or event.

However, studies have also found that when lists of supposedly random words are constructed around a theme, like our one which is 'sleep' heavy, a related word can be planted in participants' minds, so that around half of them will innocently offer it when asked to recall the words in the list.

'Confabulators' mix up things that really happened to them with things that never did. (Sometimes, head injuries to the part of the brain responsible for memory can reproduce this effect.) They can easily confuse things that they read about with things that they remember.

Sarajevo airport

Too easy? Try this list now

... airport
Sarajevo
tarmac
Bosnia
welcoming ceremony
little girl
flowers
President

Now ask yourself (without looking above)

Was the word' sniper' in the list?
Was the word 'running'?
How about 'danger'? Or even 'flak jacket'?

Hard to imagine mixing them up, but Hillary Clinton managed to do so, while she was campaigning to become candidate for the post of President of the United States. Hillary movingly described the fear of her arrival in Sarajevo, of donning protective vests against possible snipers before running across the airport tarmac to cover. Such was the kind of courage 'under fire' a presidential candidate needs to demonstrate. And the picture she painted made a powerful image. Only, the trouble is, it never really happened. TV pictures of the occasion show Hillary marching at a leisurely pace over the tarmac, accompanied by her teenage daughter, to a group of dignitaries including a seven-year-old girl who curtsies and gives the intrepid Hillary a bouquet of flowers.

Hillary explained the discrepancy later as a mere lapse in memory: 'Why, I speak millions of words a day!' she said. But it would have been perhaps more plausible to explain that she has a problem distinguishing events in the real world from events in the many imaginary ones. Having heard about the dangers of snipers in Bosnia, and seen images of people scuttling across airports from planes to buildings, perhaps in her memory she confused the various elements, and became a 'confabulator'.

Day 12

Jargon for Dummies

Philosophers don't talk much about management which is a pity. And if Adam Smith was writing today, his 1776 bestseller *An Inquiry into the Nature and Causes of the Wealth of Nations* would have to compete with even better-selling works such as *First, Break All the Rules: What the World's Greatest Managers Do Differently*, written by 'two consultants for the Gallup Organization', Marcus Buckingham and Curt Coffman. Buckingham and Coffman culled their observations from more than 80,000 interviews conducted by Gallup, in order to 'debunk some dearly held notions about management', and offer up in their place 'four keys' to working with, or rather over, people. These are:

- put everyone in jobs that suit them;
- build on their strengths;
- identify everyone's aims;
  (and finally)
- assess people in terms of *talent* – not just knowledge and skills.

For example, if someone is not very good at some aspect of their work, rather than try to overcome this defect, why not simply team them up with someone naturally good at whatever it is? Then the first person is able to 'concentrate on their strengths'.

Buckingham and Coffman put it rather nicely, 'white-board' style:

People don't change that much.
Don't waste time trying to put in what was left out.
Try to draw out what was left in.

That's hard enough.

This is inspirational stuff. Or is it, as one Amazon reader puts it, that the Gallup Organization is 'yet another tedious pop psychology outfit, setting itself up with all the credibility and authority to infiltrate society and tinker around with human thinking'?

And anyway, Smith put it rather better all those years ago, in his description of the manufacture of a simple pin. Acting alone, he says, one man could 'scarce, with his utmost industry, make one pin a day, and certainly could not make twenty'. But if the work can be divided up:

> one man draws out the wire, another straights it, a third cuts it, a fourth points it, a fifth grinds it at the top for receiving the head; to make the head requires three distinct operations; to put on is a peculiar business, to whiten the pins is another; it is even a trade in itself to put them into the paper.

Then he suggests, ten people could produce 'about twelve pounds of pins a day', adding that

> there are in a pound upwards of four thousand pins of middling size. Those ten persons, therefore, could make upwards of forty-eight thousand pins a day. But if they had all wrought them separately, ... they could certainly not each of them made twenty, perhaps not one pin a day.

Smith then goes on to relate this advantage to various money-making matters, but he also recognises its social and human implications.

Adam Smith and the job maketh the man

If the process of the division of labour is *desirable* in economic terms, in social terms, Smith has his doubts ... People are all much of a muchness, although jobs make the man. When the philosopher and the beggar, for example, came into the world, 'neither their parents nor their play-fellows could perceive any remarkable difference'. But pity the factory worker. He 'has no occasion to exert his understanding or to exercise his invention ... He naturally loses, therefore the habit of such exertion, and generally becomes as stupid and ignorant as it is possible for a human creature to become.' The factory hand, performing a monotonous simple task allotted by the logic of the division of labour, becomes equally monotonous and simple-minded.

Smith sees the state as having a responsibility to counter the *undesirable* effects of the division of labour through a programme of compulsory education, as well as (like Plato) through ensuring public entertainments are of an uplifting kind. His laissez-faire approach does not extend to education, where, for a 'very small expence the publick can facilitate, can encourage and can even impose upon almost the whole body of the people, the necessity of acquiring those most essential parts of education'.

Day 13

Be Lucky!

Why was there such a big difference between the time taken by the 'lucky' group and that taken by the unlucky ones to count newspaper photographs? It was because the second page of the newspaper contained the prominent announcement: 'Stop counting – There are 43 photographs in this newspaper.'

Anyone spotting this was saved a lot of bother. But the unlucky ones tended not to spot it as they worked slowly through the pages.

Wiseman says this shows that unlucky people are less able to spot opportunities than their fortunate companions. It is part of his general theory that discerns certain key characteristics for being lucky, all of which are possible to learn.

1   Create and spot opportunities.
2   Allow chance (or is it really your subconscious?) to work for you by using your 'intuition'.
3   Create positive outcomes by starting with positive expectations.
4   Turn bad luck into good by being tenacious and persistent.

Of course, it might just prove that misfortune dogs some people in every-thing, and that by sheer bad luck they (for example) flipped too quickly over the page that had the announcement – or started looking at the opposite end to which it would eventually appear. Another explanation, and a possible example of experimental bias, is that sports pages in the UK are always at the back of papers and sports fans therefore tend to always read papers 'backwards'. Such people can be seen on trains opening their newspapers and immediately flipping them round to the back page. By putting the announcement on page 2, Wiseman assumed a sort of philosophical, indeed logical, approach that discriminated against these sporty types. And what sort of people are these anyway? Surely an unlucky kind of person, lacking the sophistication to read the real news. However we digress. In any case, there is no such bias here. Our announcement is plonked right in the middle of the book. So we can tell at once who are the lucky people.

Assuming that luck is more a matter of attitude than events makes sense, as events tend to occur in chains (except when they are fatal …). For example, a young philosopher might have a new boss who decides to make everyone in the department take a logic test. This is unfortunate, particularly if you do not in fact know any logic and consider the study of psychology (and luck) to give more philosophical insights instead.

The bad luck might then be compounded by being first sacked and then remaining unemployed for several years. During this time the stress might make you ill and the cat might be left out late at night and get into fights with Ginger Tom. All this, assuredly would be bad luck. However, the ripples in the pond spread wider too. After several years of unemploy-ment, you might become instead a writer or artist whose fame spreads from land to land. You might then retire early and live in luxury in a villa in the Pacific (or better, just by it) with our beautiful companion (dog, cat or person to taste) while back in rainy Britain the now rigorously logical department is reshuffled by the university authorities and is merged with theology. Everyone is obliged to teach creationism. Woe! So was it really bad luck to have been booted out earlier? Such judgements become arbitrary.

Another curious factor is that people judge luck not by outcome but by expectation. For instance, psychologists have found that amongst Olympic champions, those second placed are not necessarily more content than those who came in third, despite on the face of it having done better. On the contrary, the silver medallists focus on the gold medal so near and yet so far, ruing their lack of that little bit more speed or whatever, whilst the bronze medallist is very pleased with their lot, thinking of how they might easily have come in fourth and got nothing at all.

Day 14

This Is Not a Self-Help Book

This is not a self-help book. *Summarise it for yourself.*

Day 15

The Upside-down Goggles

Apart from the obvious practical dangers in such experiments (e.g., spilling hot water from the kettle, being run over, being stopped by the police and asked why you are wearing upside-down goggles while driving, the curious result is that people actually find it quite easy to adapt to seeing everything upside down. In fact, within a very few days, it makes absolutely no difference. George Stratton himself, having made some glasses, found this.

If people were 'comically helpless' at first, after a few days of always wearing the goggles, they soon ceased to be confused at all. Some demonstrated this by skiing and others by riding bicycles through city traffic while wearing the goggles. As Professor Dennett says, the 'natural (but misguided) question to ask is: did the people in the experiment adapt by mentally turning their upside-down world back right side up, or did they adapt by getting used to life in an upside down world?'

Mind Games: 31 Days To REDISCOVER Your Brain, Martin Cohen © 2010 John Wiley & Sons Inc

Being a philosopher, Dennett then explains (having just posed it) that this is the *wrong* question. In fact, he goes on, the more the subjects of the experiment adapted to the goggles, the more they reported that the question seemed irrelevant. The conclusion was that the sense of what you are seeing is inseparable from the use that is being made of it, or as Dennet phrases it, from the 'cognitive interpretation' of it.

Psychologists, being psychologists, have forced various members of the animal kingdom to wear the spectacles and measured their reactions. They found that monkeys coped well, but rats and fish struggled. Their important conclusion was that for some animals what they see depends on whether they are wearing upside-down-glasses or not.

Fire-walking and Cold Baths

Actually, fire-walking as a ritual has been practised by people from all parts of the world for thousands of years. The first written reference to fire-walking appears in a story from India dating back to 1200 BC. Since then, it has been observed and recorded as an organised event in numerous cultures and religions.

And although it continues to be looked upon by some people as a paranormal activity, it has been fairly well understood and explained using the principles of physics since the 1930s.

In the 1930s, the Council for Psychical Research in London organised two fire-walks to study the phenomenon. For the first, an Indian named Kuda Bux and two British scientists tiptoed quickly across a 12-foot fire pit, containing red-hot oak embers (that is, embers at about 800 degrees Fahrenheit). Two years later, this time led (for some reason history has left obscured) by a Muslim gentleman and an eminently unspiritual Englishman, Reginald Adcock, several others undertook a second fire-walk. In Adcock's team, *there were no survivors.*

Correction! In fact, despite lacking, indeed boasting of having no supernatural powers or assistance, none of the participants in either team was 'substantially burned', whatever that means. Anyway, it evidently meant enough for the Council for Psychical Research to issue a statement declaring that religious faith and supernatural powers were unnecessary for fire-walking, and that rather the secret lay in the low 'thermal conductivity' of wood or coal embers, together with the small amount of time that the participants' feet are in contact with them.

After this, fire-walking lost much of its interest to psychical researchers, let alone anyone else, although it experienced a small resurgence in the 1960s amongst hippies, and then in the 1980s amongst business executives (probably the same people, grown older). Both of these groups evidently saw in it a way of developing the power of the 'collective mind' over that of the individual will.

A much easier way to do the same thing is to take a cold bath. Although this too does not require any special religious convictions, it has its own ritual significance.

R-pentomino

The first person to explore the mysteries of dotty pictures was the British mathematician John Horton Conway in the 1970s. To start with he used a Chinese 'Go' board, which consists of a large grid of squares and several hundred black and white counters. He placed the black counters in the middle to make a shape, and applied the 'rules', using the white ones to avoid confusion as to which counters survived into the next generation.

Most of the patterns actually are quite easy to work out – they collapse rapidly into a handful of less interesting but stable shapes made up of just a few dots (the 'blinker', the 'traffic light', the 'beehive', and so on – see Box on page 102). But one shape with just five elements was quite different. Its discoverer, the proud Professor Conway, called it the R-pentomino, and found its behaviour to be 'wildly unstable', with each generation quite different from its predecessor. In fact, some mathematical molecules take thousands of generations to eventually settle down! But the most intriguing thing about R-pentomino is that while it is alive, it ejects into its two-dimensional world a series of dotty formations that 'glide' slowly away from the original pattern forever. In this sense, the R-pentomino is not only a wild pattern, but an immortal one too.

Conway soon decided it would be better to employ a computer to carry out the simple but repetitious calculations, and indeed there are many fascinating versions of the 'Life Game', as it is known, available on the Internet. But at a minimum, a large piece of paper drawn with a grid, plus about 50 cut-out paper counters will do. (With regard to our shape, the next generation will see all but one of the existing dots survive, as each of them has either two or three neighbours. The exception is the dot in the middle, with four neighbours. It will vanish. However, to make up, three new dots appear in each of the 'corners'.)

The 'Game of Life', to give it its proper name, was actually a development of an idea sketched in the 1940s by John von Neumann, who has a particular role in the development of the computer. And in fact, given the coincidental development and spread of computers perfectly capable of calculating the otherwise mind-bogglingly trivial calculations for various arrangements, it soon became a cult – and a keystone in the world of artificial intelligence. The game can even be adjusted to act as a kind of 'Turing Machine' – that is, a computer with a very simple structure (envisaged by another influential figure in the development of computers, Alan Turing), capable of tackling huge questions such as … the origins and meaning of 'life'.

Life patterns

The essential characteristics of life were identified in the twentieth century by a mathematician – not a biologist! – John von Neumann. These are:

- a blueprint (the DNA in all human cells)
- a factory (the mechanism that caries out the preproduction)
- a controller (to ensure that the factory sticks to the plans – in biology, this role is taken by specialised enzymes)
- a copying machine (to pass on the instructions to the next generation).

John von Neumann observed that all of these can easily be represented as logical rules, and indeed that is what J. H. Conway's game does.

Simple molecules in the 'Game of Life'

the 'blinker'

it moves – but not very much. In fact, it just 'blinks'.

the 'block'

Once a block – always a block. Unless that is, hit by a 'glider'.

the 'glider'

After being created, the glider shuffles diagonally away ... perhaps one day to meet another glider and form a new R-pentomino.

the 'beehive'

A dull but stable shape. In this world, for most life forms, the after-life is reincarnation as a beehive.

In living organisms, complexity emerges as the result of simple chemical reactions following certain rules. It is these more complex molecules that build up to become cells, and these cells which in turn interact to become specialised organs. Organs interact to form organisms which interact, communicate and reproduce on ever higher scales to form, eventually, the universe.

Day 18

Proprioception and the McGurk Effect

Proprioception is a supposed additional sense, which allows us to deter-mine the things which belong to us, like our fingers, from those that don't, like our gloves. The brain has an image of ourselves – our mouth is enormous – which guides our actions and reactions. But sometimes, perhaps after damage to the brain, this sixth sense can be lost. In such cases, people regularly experience the sensation of the separation of their soul from their body in the same sort of way as others have reported 'out of body experiences' – perhaps while lying in bed asleep or in the hospital operating theatre undergoing an operation. The mind 'sees' the body afresh, as something now separate – alien – from it.

To those who suffer the loss of proprioception, it is as if their body has died. Any relief at the soul's survival is limited by it being tied to a dead body. Now philosophers often start, like Descartes, by considering their own physical bodies. Can I doubt that this hand is mine, they ask? But to *really* doubt it is no joke …

And Descartes observed, rightly, that in a dream one can imagine that one's leg, say is covered in yellow fur, even if it is not. Descartes asks us to retreat into our innermost self (the pineal gland, he suggests tenta-tively) from whence to regard all the other parts with suspicion. The mind can be tricked in many ways about the body, therefore knowledge of ourselves is indeed doubtful. But philosophers, being practical chaps, have not asked what it means when the body is tricked about the mind.

In our nose-scratching test, it is necessary to be blindfolded because the eyes provide an alternative route for the brain to create its image of the body. And so, for people who have suffered through disease or acci-dent the loss of this peculiar sixth sense, there may be an alternative way of rebuilding control of their bodies – through observation. Dr Sacks again, describing one of his patients:

'She had, at first, to monitor herself by vision, looking carefully at each part of her body as it moved, using an almost painful conscientiousness and care. Her movements, consciously monitored and regulated, were at first clumsy and artificial, in the highest degree. But then … her movements started to appear more delicately modulated, more graceful, more natural (though still wholly dependent on use of the eyes) ... three months later I was startled to see her sitting very finely – too finely, statuesquely, like a dancer in mid-pose. And soon I saw her sitting was indeed a pose, consciously or automatically adopted and sustained, a sort of forced or wilful or histrionic posture, to make up for the continuing lack of any genuine, natural posture. (*The Man Who Mistook His Wife for a Hat*, 1985)

Sacks's patient had recovered the ability to use her body, but did she feel she 'owned' it? Alas not. She remained a 'disembodied spirit', a walking statue – even a zombie. (Curiously, health faddists can inadvertently achieve a similar failure of the proprioception circuits by excessive intake of vitamin B6. In this case, the situation returns to normal when the diet returns to normal.)

Another kind of dysfunction also involves the loss of ability to control parts of the body. People may believe that an arm or a leg is either not theirs, or that it is theirs but dead. Sacks describes a lady who not only was born blind, but had gone through her whole life without being able to use her hands. They sat in her lap 'like putty'. In this case, when her food was put slightly out of reach, leaving her to become a little hungry and impatient, the lady 'discovered' the use of her hands through an 'involuntary' attempt to reach out and grab her food!

The McGurk effect

Almost all adults, 98 per cent, at least according to the original Harry McGurk experiment (described in the science journal *Nature* back in 1976), insist that they are hearing 'DA DAA! DAAA! DA DAA! DAAA!' (itself a popular pop song not so long ago – was it the mid 1970s?. I forget though who sang it and there probably is no important scientific reason to re-listen to the record.) Anyway, Harry and his friend say the trick is the result of the brain trying to make sense of the conflicting visual and auditory cues. The brain's solution to conflicting inputs is to offer a 'fused response': 'DA DAA! DAAA! DA DAA! DAAA!'

(a.m.)

Go for a Long Walk on the Much Too Long Coastal Path

In a sense, we are all 'Flat-landers'. Philosophers long ago elevated ideal shapes, 'simple truth' and 'elegance in theory' over messy irregularity by saying these are the key to understanding the world around us. So nowadays we believe we all live on a large flat piece of paper, and what is more, when we go anywhere we do so in sensible geometric lines or curves. This is very reassuring.

As far as the coastal path goes, although it is possible to imagine search teams becoming confused if they tried to find someone located only by their distance along the path, this is a theoretical problem more than a practical one. In our everyday, organised world, there are all those collectively agreed landmarks and it would probably be very easy to say where we are by reference to them, just as we can tell someone on the other side of the world that we live under the radio pylon in Eggbuckland, near Exeter, Devon, or on Mount Coolum, near Maroochydore, Australia, without worrying about the 2-D, let alone the 3-D, details.

But in fact, in many ways we are more like, say, dust mites living on a ball of twine. From the point of view of the owner of such a ball of twine, it is a sphere with a tiny dust mite crawling along it. If the dust mite (perhaps, using a dust-mite portable phone) calls them to ask for help on their long walk, then they will want to know the dust mite's position in three-dimensions.

But for the dust mite, looking at things from close up, the twine does not seem like a complicated structure tangled up in three-dimensional space. As far as the mite is concerned, the twine simply seems to stretch away straight ahead and straight behind. It hardly makes any difference to them whether (from the human owner's perspective) the twine is neatly rolled up, or whether it has become snagged on a nail so that all the rest of the twine has dropped away forming a line. Because, for a dust mite, its position is the same whether the twine is rolled up in a ball or whether it is stretched out. The mite's location is given in one-dimensional space only – simply by saying where it is on the line of twine.

As Benoit Mandelbrot pointed out in *The Fractal Geometry of Nature* (1982), this realisation that mathematical position can depend on the relationship of the object to the observer undermines the apparent objectivity of geometry itself.

(p.m.)
Make a Bed of Nails

The mysterious ability of the Indian fakirs (and nowadays many other eccentrics too) to sleep on beds of nails is another well-documented episode in the timeless battle between 'mind' and 'matter'. So, in order to discover whether there is any 'supernatural' explanation required, what more certain and eminently practical method than to simply construct your own bed of nails and try to sleep on it overnight yourself?

Alas, for those of us who have no intention of trying it, but fortunately for those who do, it turns out that sleeping on beds of even really rather nasty-looking nails has more to do with the physical laws relating to surface area and pressure than it has to do with spiritualism and transcending reality.

Indeed, the distinguished contemporary physics professor, Dave Wiley, uses a bed of nails (when he is not fire-walking) at the specifications given here, to entertain his classes. He even embellishes the performance by having a second nail-studded plank placed over his chest (thereby creating a kind of a human sandwich) – and then having a concrete block smashed on it while he is lying there. After all, as he points out, 'Nothing will grab a kid's attention more than if teacher is going to kill themselves.'

In this way, the experiment illustrates the power of a bed of nails over the mind, rather than the reverse.

Day 20

Now Getting Really Rather Dangerous …

But these webcams are in their way too interesting to be interesting. We want ones that are much more dull. And it seems the very first webcam was created slightly ahead of the World Wide Web itself for the computer nerds of Cambridge University. They had the supremely dull idea (but then this is Cambridge) of focusing a camera on a coffee pot so that they could see from the comfort of their office whether the coffee was brewed yet. The 'Trojan Room Coffee Pot' was screen-tested in 1991, went global in 1993 and finished eight years later in August 2001 by being auctioned online for £3,350 (which is in itself a very boring fact).

But coffee pots have to compete with webcams focused on birds' nests, which recreate the esoteric pleasure of a day spent 'twitching' for all those people who otherwise might miss it. Hencam, for instance, which went online in the dreary north of England in the dreary summer of 2005 showed various hens in a Bradford chicken coop, clucking, pecking, hatching out eggs – the lot! 'I can't honestly believe so many people would want to sit around and watch hens,' said its owner to a newspaper. And some would find it hard to imagine why someone would put a camera in their hen coop too.

Doodle

Medicine is preoccupied with deficiency, and loss. It is much less well prepared to cope with excesses of any kind – too much optimism as opposed to depression, too rapid a response to stimuli as opposed to inability to respond. In 1885, Gilles de la Tourette identified a syndrome which now bears his name, in which there is an excess of nervous energy characterised by tics, grimaces, strange humour, silly tricks or antisocial behaviour of all kinds. Tourette identified the problem as the loss of control of the ego to primitive impulses. In that sense, it is a little bit like being drunk.

In the 1920s, an epidemic of 'sleepy-sickness' also puzzled European medicine. The first symptoms were akin to Tourettte's syndrome, with uncontrollable movements and convulsions, followed by an all-enveloping trance-like stupor.

Good ol' Dr Sacks treated patients who had been 'asleep' like this for 40 years with a drug called L-DOPA, which facilitates the transmission of electrical signals within the brain. This awoke the patients successfully, but frequently they went on to become over-active, prone to wild and uncontrollable impulses, even frenzies.

In some of its worse physical effects, Tourette's syndrome is like Parkinson's disease, but it has wider, more 'psychological' effects too, such as heightened responses to music, to sexual attraction, to boredom. One of Dr Sacks's patients (a simple farmhand from Puerto Rico, who he calls Miguel O.) excelled at ping-pong, with lightening reaction times coupled with extraordinary, improvised strategies. When Dr Sacks asked him to reproduce, by way of a test, a simple drawing of a square with a circle in the centre of it, and a cross in the centre of the circle, he rapidly transformed the dull square (and the cross) into a kite, and the circle into the face of an enthusiastic stick man holding on to a lavishly swirling kite-string. However, at work he was rude and unreliable. It seemed that he had to choose between sobriety and reliability, or a range of exceptional abilities coupled with a disgraceful sense of humour. When given the same drawing test while on his medication, the patient drew … a simple drawing of a square with a circle in the centre of it, and a cross in the centre of the circle.

The eventual solution was to allow this patient to take his medication during the working week, and to be 'ill' – 'hyper' – at the weekend.

Normality

> What a paradox, what an irony ... that inner life may lie dull and dormant unless released, awakened, by an intoxication or a disease ! ... We are in strange waters here, where all the usual considerations may be reversed – where illness is normal, and normality illness ...
> (Oliver Sacks, *The Man Who Mistook His Wife for a Hat*, 1985)

Cocaine, like the treatment for various recognised brain disorders, raises the levels of dopamine in the brain. It induces a sense of heightened awareness, of euphoria in those who take it, but it remains, as Freud himself put it, in no way different from the 'normal' euphoria of the healthy person.

(a.m.)

Molyneux's Problem

This problem has been pondered by many distinguished thinkers, in varying forms (often the problem of recognising colours is posed) with varying conclusions. Locke himself believed that sight and touch were entirely different sense perceptions and thus the blind man would not distinguish the sphere from the cube on first having his sight restored.

Cube

Mind Games: 31 Days To REDISCOVER Your Brain, Martin Cohen © 2010 John Wiley & Sons Inc

As he puts it in *An Essay Concerning Human Understanding*:

> I agree with this thinking gentleman, whom I am proud to call my friend, in his answer to this problem; and am of opinion that the blind man, at first sight, would not be able with certainty to say which was the globe, which the cube, whilst he only saw them; though he could unerringly name them by his touch, and certainly distinguish them by the difference of their figures felt. This I have set down, and leave with my reader, as an occasion for him to consider how much he may be beholden to experience, improvement, and acquired notions, where he thinks he had not the least use of, or help from them.

However, despite this splendid shared assessment of Mr Molyneux and Mr Locke, the experiment runs into the problem that most people asked about it assume the contrary, a finding that really rather challenges the point of it as a thought experiment which, after all, is supposed to clarify issues by direct appeal to intuitions. Instead, as Locke notes, 'this observing gentleman' advised him that 'having, upon the occasion of my book, proposed this to divers very ingenious men, he hardly ever met with one that at first gave the answer to it which he thinks true, till by hearing his *reasons* they were convinced.'

(p.m.)

Mary's Room

This experiment was considered so interesting by the BBC that they made it into a three-part documentary series called *Brainspotting*. This was full of shots of sunny Australian countryside and interviews with Frank explaining in dry lecturer style that, first of all, if Mary does learn something new, it shows that what philosophers nowadays dub *qualia* (the subjective, qualitative properties of experiences) exist. If Mary gains something after she leaves the room – if she acquires knowledge of a particular thing that she did not possess before – then that knowledge, Jackson argues, is knowledge of the *qualia* of seeing red. Therefore, it must be conceded that *qualia* are real properties, since there is a difference between a person who has access to a particular *quale* and one who does not.

That at least, is Frank Jackson's initial conclusion.

> It seems just obvious that she will learn something about the world and our visual experience of it. But then it is inescapable that her previous knowledge

was incomplete. But she had all the physical information. *Ergo* there is more to have than that, and Physicalism is false. ('Epiphenomenal Qualia', *Philosophical Quarterly*, 32 [1982])

If, upon seeing her first real tomato after years trapped in the black and white room, Mary's subjective sensation of 'redness' is different from her recognition of grey tomatoes on the old TV, then she is like someone who tastes a good cup of leaf tea after years of drinking tea made from teabags. There is a uniting of abstract, theoretical knowledge with kinaesthetic, sensational awareness. However, our old friend, Daniel Dennett, argues *au contraire*, that Mary would not, in fact, learn something new if she stepped out of her black and white room to see the colour red. But then, he is a professor.

Frank himself was sufficiently perturbed by this kind of counter-argument that in later years he agreed that Mary would, after all, not learn anything from seeing a red tomato. The 'intuition' that he himself had earlier that she might do so is now understood to be no more than a psychological curiosity. Naturally, nowadays Frank, too, is a professor!

Einstein and the relativity of perception

Einstein himself explained in 1938 that 'physical concepts are free creations of the human mind, and are not, however it may seem, uniquely determined by the external world'. He went on to offer a metaphor to explain the problem:

> In our endeavour to understand reality we are somewhat like a man trying to understand the mechanism of a closed watch. He sees the face and the moving hands, even hears its ticking, but he has no way of opening the case. If he is ingenious he may form some picture of a mechanism which could be responsible for all the things he observes, but he may never be quite sure his picture is the only one which could explain his observations. He will never be able to compare his picture with the real mechanism and he cannot even imagine the possibility or the meaning of such a comparison. (Einstein, *The Evolution of Physics*, 1938)

Unable To See Change

Ridiculous supposition? Well maybe – but consider the strange case of Frodo and the yellow jumper … !

An important investigation in human psychology is the 'narrowness' of perception – how little of all the information the senses receive actually makes its way through to the consciousness. And a related investigation ideally suited to the advent of the Internet, is that of so-called 'continuity errors' in movies. These are trivial things such as the leading lady having a freckle on her nose in one scene, not in the next, and two in the final scene! Or it might be totally overcast one minute while the lovers were kissing in the park, and bright sunshine the next. And not just seem that way! Or the director's jumper might be left on the chair. Production teams include people whose job is specifically to make sure that what is in one part of the movie remains the same even when scenes are filmed several days apart.

However, even these expert 'change-detectors' often fail to notice the continuity errors, and thus Internauts are provided with hours of harmless emailing..

In *The Return of the King*, the final film in *Lord of the Rings* trilogy, for example, one website recounts what happened after four hobbits are seen entering the Grey Havens. It explains carefully that one of them, Sam, is wearing a yellow vest with brown buttons over a white shirt. The vest can still be seen when Sam and Frodo hug. But when Frodo makes his way onto the ship and turns back to smile at his friends, Sam is no longer wearing the yellow vest. *Nor is the vest there when the three hobbits leave the Grey Havens.* But worst of all, in the homecoming scene, when Sam returns to the Shire and is reunited with his daughter, the yellow vest is back! The daughter can be hugged to it. Astonishing that such errors can be overlooked …

Life stories

'We have, each of us, a life-story, an inner narrative – whose continuity, whose sense, is our lives. It might be said that each of us
constructs and lives a 'narrative' and that this narrative is us, our
identities. Or so wrote Dr Sacks in 1985 ('A Matter of Identity',
in *The Man Who Mistook His Wife for a Hat and Other Clinical
Tales*).

Biologically, we are not so different. It is only in our personal
narratives that we discover our identities. Some people start their
life story with tales of misfortune and repression, burdens imposed
and opportunities lost. Others start it with reports of special opportunities, exceptional abilities, and good fortune. Whether the 'real'
histories were really so far apart – or even reversed – is of no matter.
Such narratives have their own logic. The individual plays out a role
determined by their life 'story', not by any crude physical fact.

'Experience is not possible until it is arranged iconically; action
is not possible unless it is organised iconically', adds Dr Sacks.
Indeed, the human mind processes not 'raw sense date', but symbols,
icons, human constructions from out of the shapeless world.

Cascade Theory

The 'three lines' may seem like a cheap trick. And it may not even work!
But try forcing a consensus on some other issues ... like:

- low fat diets reduce heart disease.
- increased CO_2 emissions cause higher global temperatures, or
- the series of *Harry Potter* books about a boy wizard is great fun for
  all ages, but especially children, and a jolly good read. It makes a very
  suitable present ...

... and people soon give in. In fact, the 'correct', 'rational' reaction to all
three questions would be 'strongly disagree'. *But don't take my word for it.*

Certainly, in real life, a quite different consensus has built up around all three, so that now most people will instead 'strongly agree'. Or maybe not so much with the Harry Potter books. (But millions of people still buy them ... or see the films!)

Social scientists call it cascade theory. The idea is that information cascades down the side of an 'informational pyramid' – like a waterfall. How many waterfalls really do cascade down pyramids? Not many. But that is not the point. It is easier for people, if they do not have either the ability or the interest to find out for themselves, to adopt the views of others. This is without doubt a useful social instinct. As it has been put, cascade theory reconciles 'herd behaviour' with rational choice because it is often rational for an individual to rely on information passed on to them by others.

Unfortunately it is less rational to follow wrong information, and that is what can often happen. We find people cascading uselessly like so many wildebeest fleeing a non-existent lion in many everyday ways. A lot of economic activity and business behaviour, including management fads, the adoption of new technologies and innovations, not to mention the vexed issues of health and safety regulation, reflects exactly this tendency of the herd to follow poor information.

Some people say that what is needed in response is to encourage a range of views to be heard, even when they are annoying to the 'majority'. Like, for instance, to allow people to 'deny' global warming. Or to let teachers in schools and universities decide what they are going to teach. But more say what is needed is stricter control of information to stop 'wrong views' being spread. It is that view that is cascading down the pyramid now.

Propaganda

In the words of Freud's nephew (day-job, theatre promoter) Edward Bernays (1891–1995) human wants and desires are 'the steam that make the social machine work' (*Propaganda*, 1928). Properly handled, the pressure of public opinion can be controlled as if 'actuated by the pressure of a button'.

The herd, he noted, liked to follow the example of a trusted authority figure. Failing that, it relied on 'clichés, pat words or images which stood for a whole group of ideas or experiences'.

One of the best examples of cascade theory is that of the entirely false consensus that built up in the 1970s around the danger of 'fatty foods'. In fact, this consensus still exists – but has never had any medical or scientific basis.

The theory can be traced back in this case to a single researcher called Ancel Keys, who published a paper in 1953 saying that Americans were suffering from 'an epidemic' of heart disease because their diet was more fatty than their bodies were accustomed to after thousands of years of natural evolution.

Keys added additional evidence from a comparative study of the US, Japan and four other countries. Country by country, this showed that a high-fat diet coincided with high rates of heart disease.

Unfortunately for the theory, traditional diets were not especially 'low-fat' – indeed, even the imaginary hunter-gatherers of yore, if they relied on eating their prey, would have had more fat in their diet than most people do today. As *Science* magazine pointed out, in the most relevant period of a hundred years before the supposed 'epidemic' of heart disease, Americans were actually consuming large amounts of fatty meat, so the epidemic followed a reduction in the amount of dietary fat Americans consumed – not an increase.

Keys's country by country comparison had been skewed; as critics at the time pointed out, many countries did not fit the theory (the obvious cases of France and Italy with their oily, fatty cuisines) but Keys simply excluded them. The American Heart Association, considered to be the voice of experts in this case, even issued a report in 1957 stating plainly that the fats-cause-heart-disease claims did not 'stand up to critical examination'. Even the case for there being any such epidemic was dubious too – the obvious cause of higher rates of heart disease was that people were living longer – long enough to develop heart disease. But it was too late, the cascade had started.

Three years later, the Association issued a new statement, reversing its view. The Association had no new evidence but had new members writing the report – Keys and one of his friends. The new report made the cover of *Time* Magazine, and was picked up by non-specialists at the US Department of Agriculture who then asked a supporter of the theory too draw up 'health guidelines' for them. Soon, scarcely a doctor (even if a few specialised researchers still protested) could be found prepared to speak out against such an overwhelming 'consensus'.

And all this was good enough for the highest medical officer in the United States – the Surgeon General – in 1988 to issue a doom-laden warning about fat in foods, zealously claiming that fatty foods were a health menace on a par with tobacco smoking.

It was really a pretty silly theory, and certainly not one based on good evidence. In fact, in recent years, large-scale studies in which comparable groups have been put on controlled diets (low-fat and high-fat) have found a correlation. The low-fat diet seems to be unhealthy! But no one is quite sure why.

So the next time someone says that 'all the experts agree' – even if they are philosophers! – don't be so sure that proves anything.

The appeal to orthodoxy

A widely-shared prejudice can also be cited as an authority. This is part of what Charles Mackay called 'the Madness of Crowds'.

Take 'global warming', for example. At the time of writing, 'everyone' agrees the earth is warming up, due to the build up of carbon dioxide as a result of man's burning of fossil fuels.

Tracking the world's average temperature from the late nine-teenth century, people in the 1930s realised there had been a pronounced warming trend. However, during the 1960s, scientists found that over the past couple of decades the trend had shifted to cooling. Many scientists predicted a continued and prolonged cooling, perhaps a phase of a long natural cycle or perhaps caused by human activities.

Scientists then noted that during the Middle Ages, it had been much hotter. Written accounts describe Germany in 1540 as suffering widespread forest fires and cattle dying during droughts. The Rhine in Cologne was so low that people were able to cross it on horseback while in Basel, you could walk on the stones of the river-bed with dry feet under the centre of the bridge, Other accounts record that wine had an unusually high alcohol content, so much that people lay drunk in the streets and as a result of the *Mordbrennerhysterie* there was a surge of executions of arsonists in Central Europe.

It seemed clear that temperatures had dropped significantly since then. Even so, others insisted that humanity's emission of gases would bring warming over the long run. In the late 1970s, this group's views became predominant, as it is now. But to say 'all the scientist agree' is meaningless, unless one adds a timeframe: 'This year, all the scientists agree ...'

> In reading the history of nations, we find that, like individuals, they have their whims and their peculiarities; their seasons of excitement and recklessness, when they care not what they do. We find that whole communities suddenly fix their minds upon one object, and go mad in its pursuit; that millions of people become simultaneously impressed with one delusion, and run after it, till their attention is caught by some new folly more captivising than the first. (Charles Mackay, *Memoirs of Extraordinary Popular Delusions and the Madness of Crowds* (1841))

If crude prejudices such as 'everyone knows that black people are lazy' or 'women cannot follow logical arguments'; or 'Jewish people are mean with money', et cetera, et cetera, may not be acceptable (although evidently, for all too many people, they still are), many less recognisably controversial ones are always safe to introduce: 'everyone knows that Orientals are very respectful of authority', 'everyone knows that women are more caring than men', et cetera et cetera.

Political debate revolves round this sort of 'everyone agrees' claim: 'everyone knows that high taxes discourage wealth generation'; 'everyone agrees that high social benefits create welfare dependency.' And most of all these days: 'All the scientists [those impeccable authorities] agree that mobile phones are safe' ... or that 'butter is bad for you ...' and so on.

It all goes to prove that there 'is no opinion, however absurd, which men will not readily embrace', as Schopenhauer complained – once it acquires the status of convention. This is because people are sheep, and like that fluffy beast, practise no independence of judgement whatsoever. Not for nothing did a Gallup poll in 1993 find that nearly half of Americans believed human beings had been 'created', more or less in their present form, sometime in the last 10,000 years. Which also goes to show the truth of Seneca's observation that 'Every man prefers belief to the exercise of judgement'.

Explain Yourself!

Economists assume that whilst there is a buzz of random short-term changes, the long-term trends are determined by sensible, macro-economic factors such as changes in technology or productivity or wars or new inventions. Traditionally, they assume that prices change smoothly, rather than in abrupt jumps – an assumption borrowed from the physics of movement. Yet, in fact, prices jump around in response to news or rumours. We search for patterns that are not there.

Biology, weather, stock markets – philosophers have long sought to explain the behaviour of each with just one set of rules. Heraclitus said 'all is flux', Thales, that all is water. Pythagoras said that all is mathematics. Today's followers of this tradition appeal to the advance of scientific knowledge, with its supposed quest for a grand unifying theory. Indeed, many people talk about how the various loose ends of knowledge are 'almost' completely gathered together now. Such people pooh-pooh those who speak of 'mysteries' and the unexplained.

Yet the very dry mathematician and computer scientist, John von Neumann, puts things around the other way. It is the mysteries that are paramount and permanent, and the explanations that are speculative and temporary. The sciences do not try to explain, he wrote, they hardly even try to interpret, they mainly make models.

By a model is meant a mathematical construct which, with the addition of certain verbal interpretations, describes observed phenomena. The justification of such a mathematical construct is solely and precisely that it is expected to work. (From a paper called 'Method in the Physical Sciences' 1955)

How many illustrations are there in this book?

There are exactly 28 illustrations in this book.

Investigating Un-Reason and Argument

Playing on ambiguity and the ridiculous counter-example often confuses opponents. Socrates, of course, asks a lot of similarly ridiculous questions in order to appear to win the debates in Plato's dialogues. And quibbles are such a powerful tool in arguments that even Zeus himself, was apparently not above using them. In one of Aesop's fables the King of Mount Olympus had promised to give the bee a wish and so when she asked that henceforth her sting be fatal, he had to agree, but neglected to clarify that it would be fatal to her. This sort of humbuggery, as Schopenhauer says, goes a long way.

Another way to triumph is to 'short-circuit' your opponent's views, and then draw a conclusion from your misinterpretation which can be thrown back. For example, the discussion of time with reference to Zeno could be short-circuited by saying 'Well, if you think time does not exist, can you explain how you always manage to catch the train home?'

Or consider this debate about Kant's ethics.

OPPONENT: It is always wrong to treat a person as a means to an end, rather than as an 'end' in themselves.

YOU: If you think it is always wrong, how is is possible for you to ask people in shops and restaurants to serve you?

If the position was reversed, and we had claimed that it was wrong to treat a person as a means to an end, rather than as an 'end' in themselves, only to be faced with opposition, we could ask 'Well, if you think it is all right to treat people as a means to an end, why don't you just kneel down there and lick my shoes clean right now?'

It's cheap, but effective.

Other weasel tactics to 'win' arguments

Tactic 1 Weasels and escape routes   Suppose we have been caught out making a factual point that we cannot back up, even by inventing statistics.

Rather than back down, or withdraw the point, it is often better to seek safe refuge in generalities.

For example, perhaps we have opined that tennis is good for the health, and been brought up sharply by a detailed account of health problems associated with tennis – heart attacks, elbow problems et cetera. To avoid conceding, it is preferable to retreat to lofty generalities about 'exercise' in general. 'Taken in moderation', we may say, 'tennis, like all cardio-vascular exercises [add in some jargon] can [use a weasel word] be benefi-cial for the health, although obviously, when taken to excess, there are health disadvantages too.'

In this way, you can retrieve an otherwise unsaveable situation. In effect, we concede the point but pretend that our opponents point was in fact our own. This cowardly tactic often succeeds.

Adding 'weasel words' like 'can be', used here instead of 'are' which is what would make sense, is the mark of the politician. A contemporary professor of politics, Jodi Dean, recently demonstrated the tactic in noting that arguments are themselves inherently political, an attempt to impose some supposed truth on another. 'Argument, thought by some to be part of the process of democracy, is futile, perhaps [weasel] because democracy can [second weasel] bring about the Holocaust.'

A more historical use of this shameless tactic is provided by Karl Marx, who wrote an article on the likely consequences of a mutiny in India in the 1850s. He told his friend Engels later that he did not really know what might actually happen but that he had 'of course, so worded my position to be right either way'.

Tactic 2 Be too specific, confuse with irrelevant details Another device is to take a correct remark and extend it to things it is not really intended to apply to. Take, for example, an argument about old lead pipes in houses. Some fine old buildings are being condemned for demolition partly on account of the cost of replacing their pipes with modern ones. This is what happens in the debate.

OPPONENT (*correctly*): The old houses are simply too expensive to reno-vate. Lead in water is extremely dangerous and unfortunately, therefore, the old houses are not suitable for human habitation any more
YOU: The dangers of lead in water are much exaggerated. Lead is present in all soils, rivers, lakes and seawater. Don't forget, [appealing to the audience's conceit, as the audience had no idea of this but probably feel they ought to have] lead is also in the air, borne in dust and sea spray. Lead is present in the proportion of about 15 parts per million in igneous rocks, that is, the most common ancient rocks on the surface of the

Earth, and in soil. Natural soils are never lead-free. As for the houses – as long as the water is run for a few minutes every morning (to clear the pipes of the water that has been standing in them overnight) the level of lead in them is easily reduced and falls below natural background levels

OPPONENT *(flustered)*:   Ridiculous! *Any* lead is dangerous.

YOU: On the contrary, even if the lead in our water supply was removed artificially, we would still take in about half a milligram of lead a day. Where does this lead come from, you may ask? It enters the body from the air during breathing, but most of it is taken in orally, as food, drinks, drugs, supplements, indeed almost everything that is ingested. In a healthy adult, the entire body contains traces of lead, with 90 per cent of it concentrated in the bones, where it reaches levels much higher than the background level in the environment.

OPPONENT *(red faced and shouting)*:   I STILL SAY, THE LESS LEAD THE BETTER. LEAD ACCUMULATES IN THE BODY CAUSING BRAIN DAMAGE. EVERYBODY KNOWS THIS!

YOU *(reasonably*)*:   Actually, the human body eliminates lead via many mechanisms. It does not usually accumulate. Lead exits the body via faeces (mainly as the result of dietary lead not being absorbed, but also discharged via the gallbladder from breakdown of haemoglobin that binds lead); through sweat; excretion into the skin, hair, and nails; and through the urine and the breath. Except at times of unusually high lead exposure, the total lead taken into the body each day is eliminated each day.

Who wins?

Whether all this is true or not, is less important than that it sounds possible. (In this case, I understand it is true. But why believe me?) Certainly, your opponent will not know, and can only lamely retreat by saying 'Too much lead is bad for you' – which of course we can pounce on as an example of a tautology. 'Too much of anything is bad for you!' (Mae West's famous contrary opinion aside – she says it is 'marvellous').

Tactic 3 Invent categories ('label libel')   Categorising things is a powerful tool. That is Kant's view too. Or rather, that is 'the later Kant's view in the *Prolegomena*' but not 'the younger Kant's view in the *Kritik*'. Labelling something implies both that you are familiar with argument, and that is has no originality. Offering spurious references creates a cloud of supposedly scholarly dust around the issue, blinding both the opponent and the audience.

---

*   Speaking reasonably often enrages opponents in arguments. Use this tactic with care!

Note, in passing, that it is always best to refer to things as though you assume your audience knows the work, and so it is better to say 'the *Kritik*', not 'his great work, the *Critique of Pure Reason*'. In this way, you humble people into not saying 'What are you talking about?' which would expose you to charges of talking nonsense.

A popular variation on this labelling theme is to associate the opponent's view with an 'unpopular group'. You might say, for example, 'Yes, that is how the Catholic Church/the Moonies/the Nazis saw it too ...'

This strategy serves to discredit the argument, again without providing any reason.

Wikijargon

That great public debating chamber, Wikipedia on the World Wide Web, provides many excellent examples of 'label libel', using special new terms invented by the 'Wikipedians'. Views one person disagrees with are castigated as POV – which means a personal 'point of view' and hence not 'neutral' (like their own one of course). Debaters over things such as Kant's views in the later *Kritik* can be speedily brought to conclusion by declaring the opponent's views to be 'vandalism'. The dissenter will then be 'blocked' and their views 'oversighted' which is Wikijargon for 'deleted'. If only ALL debates could be so effectively controlled!

Tactic 4 Appeal to self-interest   Often the simplest way to win an argument is to appeal to either your opponent's or the audience's self-interest. If someone has said cars are bad for the environment, point out how difficult it would be to go for a picnic in the mountains or to that lovely remote beach that no one else goes to, without a car!

Save yourself time – skip the rest of the discussion!

Tolstoy once observed that 'most men, including those at ease with problems of the greatest complexity, can seldom accept even the simplest and most obvious truth if it be such as would oblige them to the falsity of conclusions which they have delighted in explaining in ... to others', conclusions which they have 'woven thread by thread into the fabric of their lives'.

Tactic 5 'Humpty-Dumptying':* puzzle and bewilder by meaningless statements   Bewildering your audience usually works as people assume what you have said makes sense, and that if they are not able to follow, it is because they have either missed a bit out (not paid attention) or are simply intellectually inferior. In either case, they must remain silent and concede the advantage to you.

Victory!

Is that why people read philosophy books? Well, certainly there is a whole branch of philosophy devoted to the study of this tactic, which we may call called 'post-rationalism'. It encompasses post-modernism, critical theory, post-structuralism and so on, all various made up names for nothing so much as playing with words. That would not be so bad, if the words were amusing or 'playful'. They are just very, very dull. Take for example, the work of one of the school's greatest exponents, Gilles Deleuze (from whom we get the word 'delusion' ... or at least, ought to). 'In the first place', Gilles commences,

> singularities-events correspond to heterogeneous series which are organised into a system which is neither stable nor unstable, but rather metastable', endowed with a potential energy wherein the differences between series are distributed. (*The Logic of Sense*, 2004)

He continues, if you want more (not that it is necessary):

> In the second place, singularities possess a process of auto-unification, always mobile and displaced to the extent that a paradoxical element traverses the series and makes them resonate, enveloping the corresponding singular points in a single aleatory point and all the emissions, all dice throws, in a single cast.

As the journalist Francis Wheen says, commenting on this piece of pellucid prose, 'One can gaze at this paragraph for hours and be none the wiser.' Yet, as he also notes, Deleuze is a highly respected philosopher, hailed by his fellow Frenchman, Michel Foucault, as one of the 'greatest amongst

---

*   Humpty Dumpty it was who said, from his splendid but short-lived perch on the wall, that words could mean whatever he chose them to mean.

the great'. Foucault even went so far as to predict that 'some day, the century will be Deleuzian'. This is excellent humbuggery.

Tactic 6 Simply say the opposite   Another great tactic, much used both in domestic life and in philosophical debate is to simply say the opposite of whatever your opponent (partner/parent/child) says. There is even a special name for this, 'denying the antecedent', although strictly speaking this special name applies to something completely different in logic. Anyway, we probably all know people who use this tactic, and there are three possible responses.

1   Simply repeat your point until they tire of disagreeing and give up. (This may never happen.)
2   Couch your point in ambiguous terms, so that your opponent is unable to tell what you think, and so is unable to simply adopt the opposite position.
3   Best of all, imply that you think one thing when in reality you think the opposite. If this works, your opponent makes your point for you, and you can floor the 'no-sayer' by speedily agreeing. 'Exactly!' you say very crisply.

For example, consider a debate on whether there really is a difference between 'right' and 'wrong'. Suppose we say that there is, and someone else insists on the contrary. The argument might go:

YOU: Civilisation is based on the collective recognition of the difference between right and wrong.
OPPONENT: There is no difference between right and wrong as such judgements are wholly subjective, and 'relative'.
YOU *(playing the 'Nazi card' immediately)*:   So you think there is no difference between Hitler and the people he put in the concentration camps.
OPPONENT *(who was expecting this)*:   No. Not at all! For the Nazis, the people put in the camps were all people who had committed offences, in their terms. Why, even in the bunker in the dying days of the Reich, Mrs Goebbels wrote movingly to her son of the high ethical standards of her husband and Hitler! 'Our glorious idea is in ruins, and with it everything I have known in my life that was beautiful, noble and good.'*

---

*   A good quotation is often worth its weight in gold (and how much does a 'quote' weigh? nothing!) but most of us cannot remember them. It pays to become unscrupulous in filling out those unfortunate gaps in memory to make the point more satisfactorily. But this one I have checked and is, I think, correct, as it happens.

Anyway, as our opponent appears to be winning, making more interesting points than us, we try to be more stealthy. Ambiguity is the quickest way to trip the no-sayer …

> YOU: Very well. So would you say that there were no ethical issues raised
>   by the Nazi concentration camps?
> OPPONENT: I … er … not exactly … er …

Checkmate!

This tactic works here as to say 'No, not at all. The camps did raise ethical issues', although instinctively tempting to a no-sayer, is not clearly to contradict us, and would allow us to agree with them! Disaster to a no-sayer!

On the other hand, to reply, 'Yes. The Nazi concentration camps raise no ethical issues' defies the general sense that they did, even if, as our opponent says, it is not at all clear that the Nazis themselves thought they were 'bad'. It leaves the no-sayer stranded on such difficult-to-defend ground that we can simply abandon the matter there, saying loftily, 'Well, if that is your position I do not intend to spend any further time discussing it.'

Note that none of this advances the debate. But recall that, as Schopenhauer says, demonstrating points is not the aim. The aim is victory!

Subliminal Messages

In fact, in the 1950s the power of subliminal messages seemed to be so great, and its sneakiness so bad, that the consumers rebelled. The same year, the *New Yorker* protested that 'minds were being broken and entered', while the normally calm *Newsday* referred to the contraption that Vicary used (and sold) to add subliminal messages to films as 'the most alarming invention since the atomic bomb', an assertion that must surely indicate that minds had already been broken into and damaged …

Scarcely surprising then that two attempts were made by Congress to ban the marketing technique. Both failed, doubtless due to sophisticated marketing techniques, or it could have been because Vicary proved to be unable to 'replicate' or indeed substantiate his astonishing earlier success (leading to suspicions that he had made the whole story up). However that may be, in 1973, the publication of a new alarmist book, *Subliminal Seduction,* by Dr. Wilson B. Key, identified scores of advertisements filled with hidden messages and secret symbols – including the notorious example of the word 'S-E-X' spelled out in the ice cubes in a whiskey advertisement. This showed a progression in the thinking on appeals to the subconscious mind, which now concentrated on more Freudian, not to say 'reptilian' matters. The unedifying subject matter obliged a rattled US Federal Communications Commission to finally act. In 1974, it issued a policy statement saying that 'subliminal perception' techniques were 'against the public interest' and banned them from radio and television.

That only left advertisers and marketeers with all the other methods of influencing public opinion …

Day 28

(a.m.)

The Power of Prayer

Prayer is a special kind of thought – an attempt indeed to project your thoughts. But can prayers affect events? Can mind affect matter, despite no apparent causal mechanism?

Dr Herbert Benson, of the Mind/Body Medical Institute in Boston, USA, conducted a practical experiment to settle the matter. His idea was to see if prayers had the power to cure sick people. Dr Benson seems to have been largely sympathetic to the idea that they could, and so his experiment should be taken as being an attempt to demonstrate a positive. Anyway, to start with, he divided nearly 2,000 patients recovering from major surgery into three groups. Of these three groups two were prayed for and one was left 'unprayed' for. Naturally, it might affect the results if you knew whether you were being prayed for or not, so he ensured that one group was prayed for but did not know it, one group was prayed for and did know it, and one group was not prayed for but did not know it. Actually, he neglected to have a group of patients who were not prayed for and also knew it, which would have made the set of possibilities complete. But then, I suppose patients in the absence of Dr Benson and his team are in that position anyway.

Meanwhile, the congregations of three Christian churches were given lists of patients, anonymised by being reduced to first names plus the initial letter of the family name. They were asked to say this short prayer for each person on the list: 'for a successful surgery with a quick healthy recovery and no complications'.

So much for the experiment. What were the results?

Actually, the experiment showed no difference between the recovery of those patients who were prayed for and those who were not. Curiously though, those who were aware that they were being prayed for … did rather worse.

(p.m.)

Pray for Good Crops

Many variations on this experiment have been carried out by many researchers, most of them, it must be acknowledged, religious cranks. But there are many other kinds of crank too. Anyway, there seems to be some kind of effect which is 'beyond statistical chance'. (But see the debriefing notes for Day 3 to see people's understandings of *that*.)

In a book called *Psychological Perspectives on Prayer* (2001), Leslie John Francis and Jeff Astley carefully catalogue numerous examples of plants that were given regular prayers sprouting, blooming and fruiting ahead of unloved ones. One experiment involved planting 46 corn kernels in a large seed tray, half on one side, half on the other. The corn kernels on the left side were then prayed over for every day for a week. At the end of that time, as the experimenter reported 'sixteen sturdy little seedlings greeted us on the positive side'. On the negative side? 'There was but one.' And that no doubt was probably on the boundary, but this important detail is not recorded.

Follow-up experiments involved cultivating three identical pot plants in three small plant pots. One pot plant was then prayed for regularly, the second was looked after in a material sense but not a spiritual one, while the hapless third plant was given negative prayers – it was asked to not grow any more.

A Mr Erwin Prust, of Pasadena, chose three ivy plants and following five weeks of prayers, he found that while the prayed-for plants and the 'ignored' plants' had both grown quite well, the plants receiving the negative prayers 'were now quite dead'. *Spooky or what?*

Yet how do you give negative prayers anyway? One technique described in the book is to call the seedlings 'Communists'. Under this unkind political assessment, the seedlings 'seemed to twist and writhe under the negative power showered on them', as well they might.

But there was more evidence. A larger sample involving some six teams of 'prayer-makers' and 720 seeds, all using the same procedure (three pots, one to be prayed for positively, one to be prayed for negatively, and the 'control' not prayed for at all) again showed the negative prayers having some sort of effect (although this time it is specified as what seems now to be a 'mere' 10.95 per cent)

A famous if not terribly well-documented example of the power of mind over plant-matter is described in the Bible. It occurred when a hungry Jesus came across a fig tree that he thought should have had fruit on it, but did not. Atypically, he cursed it, and sure enough within 'a matter of hours', the tree 'dried up from the roots'. Reliable observer Saint Mark records all that. The true prophet of plant prayers however is indubitably the Reverend Franklin Loehr, whose book *The Power of Prayer on Plants* (first published in 1959) is a sort of mini Bible of its own. He carried out no fewer than 700 such experiments involving 150 prayer-makers making 100,000 measurements on no fewer than 27,000 seedlings – that's a whole field full! He found that prayed-for plants not only did better than those given the negative thoughts but trumped even those left completely alone. They were said to germinate faster, to grow better, and to have more resistance to insects. Naturally, this important work merited further studies, and in fact since the 1960s there have been hundreds of so-called scientific studies involving not only plants but mice, red blood cells, yeast and even bacteria. There were even one or two more involving humans. Most unfortunately, while the religious scientists were easily persuaded of the findings, few others have been prepared to accept that the studies have really proved anything … unless that is, the credulity of man.

The Horror and the Beauty Or Vice Versa

Visions of Hildegard

Despite her early success with the cow, however, Hildegard herself was for a long time unsure of quite how much to make of the visions. They were often accompanied with fainting fits, and sometimes she experienced total loss of normal feeling: 'I do not know myself, either in body or soul. And I consider myself as nothing. I reach out to the living God and turn everything over to the Divine.'

Although she was sure that they *must* be messages from God, she opted at first to keep the details to herself. But later, after becoming increasingly ill, she decided that God was cross at her for not communicating His message to others. From then on, Hildegard explains, 'I wrote them down because a heavenly voice kept saying to me, "See and speak! Hear and write!"' Ever after that the visions were described in faithful detail, as illuminated manuscripts and as musical compositions – ethereal music in which 'echoing voices soar up and down the scales like angels singing in full flight', as one recent commentator, Paul Harrison, enthusiastically put it.

In the manuscripts, delicate images illustrate the visions, and Hildegard depicts herself as a tiny seated figure with a slate or open book, gazing upwards at huge symbolic mandalas of cosmic processes, full of angels and demons and winds and stars. The words of God are recorded in Latin, as that was apparently God's preferred human tongue at that time. In one manuscript, God explains the creation in terms of mystic energies:

'I, the highest and fiery power, have kindled every spark of life … I, the fiery life of divine essence, am aflame beyond the beauty of the meadows, I gleam in the waters, and I burn in the sun, moon, and stars. With every breeze, as with invisible life that contains everything, I awaken everything to life. The air lives by turning green and being in bloom. The waters flow as if they were alive. The sun lives in its light, and the moon is enkindled, after its disappearance, once again by the light of the sun so that the moon is again revived … And thus I remain hidden in every kind of reality as a fiery power. Everything burns because of me in the way our breath constantly moves us, *like the wind-tossed flame in a fire.* (From Hildegaard's *Symphonia armoniae celestium revelationum*, mid-twelfth century)

Such messages were often accompanied for Hildegard by a brilliant light – more brilliant than a cloud revealing the sun. Within this light there was sometimes an *even brighter one* which Hildegard called 'the living light.' This one made her lose all sadness and anxiety.

On the other hand, describing another vision, she says:

> I saw a great star most splendid and beautiful, and with it an exceeding multitude of falling stars which with the star followed southwards ... And suddenly they were all annihilated, being turned into black coals ... and cast in to the abyss so that I could see them no more.

This, she interprets as 'the Fall of the Angels'. However, there are other possible explanations. Recent more medically minded commentators, notably Dr Sacks himself, have been quick to interpret it rather as a migraine attack or a kind of 'negative scotoma', that being a disturbance of the visual processing part of the brain. At least Sacks is not totally dismissive. He says rather that this is an example of how a physiological misfortune can for some sufferers be interpreted as a kind of gift. Sacks recalls too that Dostoevsky too suffered from attacks of epilepsy, during which he felt himself to be briefly in touch with 'the eternal harmony', adding:

> a terrible thing is the frightful clearness with which it manifests itself and the rapture with which it fills you. If this state were to last more than five seconds, the soul could not endure it, and would have to disappear. During those five seconds I live a whole human existence, and for that I would give my whole life and not think that I was paying too dearly.

In a sense, dream worlds like these are also 'thought experiments', yet they are ones characterised by a blithe disregard for the usual rules of thought, drawing instead on poetry and metaphor. But that still rules out the more interesting mystical or religious explanations.

Visions of horror

Jung's dream makes an interesting vision, and refreshingly different from Hildegard's – but could it only have been his subconscious over-doing daily worries – perhaps general ones concerning starting a new job or more particular ones concerning his own research leading him away from Freud's approach to understanding the workings of the human mind?

Well, maybe. Because, of course, it is easy to dismiss dreams or even visions as random representations of emotions or feelings, And in fact, at first, Jung was concerned that his visions were predicting the onset of a psychosis, whatever that is (one would need a psychoanalyst to find out). But later, after more reflection and as a result of watching world events rapidly unfold, he came to believe that his dream had been a vision warning of the approaching world war, which would indeed begin in August of 1914.

Unfortunately, he never managed to persuade anyone to do anything about it.

Strange Things

But perhaps someone had mentioned to Miss Telbin what had been on the card that Sir William had been looking at earlier in the day.

No! With all the aplomb of a knight of the realm, Sir William adds that any explanation that the result might have been 'due to collusion between the persons experimenting' of course cannot be entertained, not least by himself, who was one of the experimenters.

It might seem, in the cold light of day, unlikely that anyone could influence real-life events by pure thought alone, whether via an intermediary (God) or directly by the mysteries of the mind.

But it still seems possible that the powers of the mind might stretch a little further than the dreary rearranging of chemicals in the brain, as the scientists (and most contemporary philosophers) insist is the case. The ancient Greek philosopher Democritus put forth an early version of the wave and corpuscle theory to explain how thought transference might work.

Yet, even if physical effects (reluctantly) have to be ruled out, might not there still be thought transference? For example, might there not be some kind of communication possible by, 'at present unknown' means – such as telepathy?

That does not seem too much to ask. After all, references are often to be found in ancient writings and oral lore and in many traditional societies, such as the Aborigines of Australia, it is accepted as a human faculty. Plus, telepathy has in fact a long philosophical pedigree. For Thomas Aquinas and others, communication is between minds, and it was only after the unfortunate 'apple-tasting' in the Garden of Eden that we were reduced to mere bodily communication.

With science back in fashion in the nineteenth century, a new kind of investigator, the British chemist and physicist William Crookes, suggested telepathy could work through radio-like brain waves. Over in America, the psychologist and philosopher William James was also very enthusiastic about the possibility of telepathy and encouraged more research be put into it. As the twentieth century opened, the Soviet scientist L.L. Vasilies unveiled a new and more sophisticated electromagnetic theory.

Sigmund Freud was not at all interested in the mechanisms, but noticed the phenomenon so often that he felt he could not ignore it in his writings on psychology. He termed it a regressive, primitive faculty that was lost in the course of evolution, but which still had the ability to manifest itself under certain conditions. His rival, Carl G. Jung thought it more important. He considered it a function of synchronicity, that strange 'non-causal' mechanism where events are nonetheless significantly linked.

Atomic telepathy

One of the minor objections to telepathy is that it appears to be offend the laws of physics by involve instantaneous communication over large distances. Twin One in Australia can know instantly that something is wrong with Twin Two in London – and the least problem is the speed at which it occurs. Yet before we modestly concede that human telepathy only seems instantaneous and in fact involves the characteristic slight delay caused by respect of the laws of physics, it should be noted that in recent years, physicists and not just para-psychologists have carried out experiments which show that under certain circumstances communication is possible at 'faster-than-light' speeds. In fact, it seems instantaneous communication is possible.

A way of detecting 'faster-than-light', not to say instantaneous, communication between the various bits of an atom, euphemistically termed as 'non-local' interaction by scientists, was proposed in the 1960s by John Bell, one of the founders of CERN, the phenomenally expensive European laboratory for the study of particle physics. It took two decades and a great deal of money before Alain Aspect used the new CERN atom crusher to demonstrate that when two photons are ejected in opposite directions from a single atom, they remain forever 'twinned', or 'entangled' as physicists prefer to put it, so that if one spins one way, the other must spin the other way. Change the state of the first, the other instantly changes its state too, as if they were one entity.

Later on, experiments seemed to find that matter which (as far as anyone knows) had completely separate origins, can also be 'entangled' in a similar way. This makes more sense when you remember that all atoms are made up of invisible particles which are spread out over the entire universe and behave like waves in a sea of energy. Because of this, respectable scientists now agree that no atom can be treated as an 'island' in the sea, far less as an 'isolated system', leaving open the possibility at least of 'instantaneous communication'.

Easier methods for telepathy

Many of the most impressive telepathic feats could be, and indeed often are, reproduced by trickery. In reading minds, sending messages through walls, predicting future events, professional magicians are often experts, as in many other arcane skills. For them, all mind-reading requires is a good memory, an ability to think fast – and many hours of rehearsal ...

The experiment: Sending a mental image of a playing card to another person in a remote location   This is one of the simplest and yet most startling illustrations of mind-reading. Here is how to do it.

First of all, gather together a group of people prepared to be impressed with your new skill. Once such a team is gathered, simply pass a deck of playing cards around the group asking them to select and agree on one card – any card – they wish. This card will be the one whose image is to be transmitted telepathically. Having (doubtless rather suspiciously) selected their card, they then pass it to you to study carefully. After a few seconds, you attempt to project the image of the card to a friend of yours with whom, as you explain, you have previously had excellent results with telepathy. Allow a few seconds during which the image is not so much sent as 'settles' in your friend's consciousness, and then announce that you have successfully transmitted the image of the card to your friend. As the group is doubtless still rather sceptical, give them your friend's name and telephone number so that they can ring your friend up and check.

Here's what happens. (*Whisper*: The card in this case was the Four of Spades.)

Drring drrring ...
VOICE: Hullo?
EXPERIMENTERS: Hullo! Is that Dr Evans?
VOICE: Yes, it is. And would you by chance be ringing about a certain playing card, an image of which has just been sent to my mind?!
EXPERIMENTERS: Extraordinary – that is exactly what we are doing! Please, can you just say what the card was?
VOICE: Why certainly: I have just received a very distinct mental image *of the Four of Spades.*

How did they do that!

This one really works, if you believe in the possibility of the transference of mental images. Or even if you don't. Because – like most professional magic ticks – it involves a very simple piece of sleight of hand. In this case, although of course the telephone number of your telepathic friend is a constant, the name you call them changes to indicate the number and suit of the card. The first letter of the name can indicate the 'number' (E corresponds to '5') and the 'title' bestowed on your shameless accomplice likewise can give away the suit (in this case, it was previously agreed that the use of 'Dr' would indicate a card from the suit of Spades.) In such simple ways can information be covertly conveyed right in front to the noses of the most alert investigators!

The magic telephone

It seems hard to imagine now, but once upon a time, the ability to talk to people at great distances through the invisible magic of telephones was as hard to accept as the kind of communication that telepathy experimenters claim.

When the famous physicist, Professor Tait, heard the news of the invention of the telephone, which was conveyed to him apparently by Morse code and electric telegram, in itself a ridiculous and implausible method, he was asked what he thought of it. He replied, 'It is all humbug, for such a discovery is physically impossible.'

Asked then how it was that many well-respected witnesses had asserted that they had heard speech transmitted across several miles by this new mechanism, Tait replied that (like the children's' game of connecting two bean cans by a piece of taut string) it was 'probably a case of the conduction of sound by long straight wires'. Indeed, the Professor continued to reject the machine even after the telephone was formally demonstrated to scientists at the British Association by Lord Kelvin, and his arguments persuaded many more to level accusations of trickery. When Edison's new 'phonograph' was exhibited in Paris, he too was accused of concealing a ventriloquist somewhere in the room and using them to send voices 'apparently' out of the confounded contraption.

The bonehead method

The experiment: Knowing the answer to sealed-up questions   Again, a small group of sceptics is required. Ask everyone to write down a question for you on a sheet of plain white paper. (Provide the pens and paper.) Then they must fold the paper twice and staple it shut. This is to prevent you looking at their questions.

To show them what you mean, write a question for yourself and fold and staple it.

After you have collected the questions in, shuffled them around a bit, you then pick one up at random. Hold the sealed-up question to the side of your head in a suitably para-psychologist manner ... while you try to 'mind read' what it says. Then you slowly, painfully even (for mind-reading is tiring and difficult), announce the answer to the still sealed-up question.

Here is what might then happen if there were four people in the group and five questions. First of all, hold the piece of paper to your head and let the question mysteriously enter into your mind. Then pronounce 'By extra sensory perception ...'

Now you unseal the paper and read the question, which, inevitably (given your powers) turns out to have been your own one which was: 'How do you manage to read sealed questions?' Then refold the paper, put it in a separate pile and pick up the next question. Repeat the misleading procedure and then announce the next answer: 'Paris.'

This is more impressive as it was not your question. Repeat the ritual unfolding and reading of the question which this time turns out was: 'What is the capital of France?' Refold the paper and add to the pile.

Hold up another piece of paper to the side of you head and say slowly: 'Snowy'.

This time the question it turns out was 'What is the name of Tintin's dog?'

Next, in similar fashion comes the short response '64', in answer to the query: 'What is four cubed?' (Someone always asks a mathematical question ...) Last answer of all is 'rhubarb tart' for: 'What is for lunch?' – another reliable evergreen by someone not taking things too seriously. Nonetheless, it is really a rather extraordinary feat, and so you should pass the papers back to the group for them to check these really were the questions and there was no trickery.

But what does the bonehead method prove?

Being 'one step ahead' is a useful trick not only for psychical researchers but for people in life in general (ask any investor – or even an 'insider dealer' – about the advantages it offers). The trick here is again very simple. Although you appeared to select your question first, you in fact made sure you did not (perhaps you stapled it differently) and so when you unfolded the first piece of paper, you were reading a 'genuine' question. This makes you 'one ahead' of the audience. You note this question mentally, but read out your own one from memory. The next time you hold the paper up to your head, it follows you actually know a real question that needs answering, although you still have no way of knowing what is on the paper. On the other hand, neither does the audience.

More codes (another cunning device for the use of codes to secretly convey information)

Experiment: Demonstrate how to send a simple piece of information to a newly trained telepathic receiver outside the room   For this you need three objects (three animal models would do well) and one (suitably co-operative) person to volunteer to be your 'receiver' for the telepathic message. Explain that telepathy can be learnt, and that you will quickly share one technique with this person. Then take them outside the room to wait. You also briefly explain the 'technique' to them.

Returning to the room, you then ask your fellow investigators to arrange the three animals in a line on the table and select one of them. For example, there might be a wooden giraffe, a china pig and a fluffy dog, arranged in that order. (*Whisper:* this time, the group selects the china pig in the middle.) You then stare at each of the three animals and transmit the image of the pig to the 'receiver' waiting outside the room. To correctly identify this animal out of the three is the test.

If the room has two doors, it is quite nice to now offer to leave the room completely. Otherwise it will probably suffice to ostentatiously stand facing the wall. Whatever, you will agree to the requirements of the group who will want to be sure that you are not physically giving any clues as to the identity of the chosen object. But just before leaving the room, or whatever, you call the receiver back.

Here is what might happen.

'All right, you can come back!'

You leave the room. The receiver enters. The three animals look suitably impassive. The 'chairman' of the investigators then says 'Which animal did we select?' The receiver then immediately either names, or points at – or both! – *to the china pig in the middle.*

This feat can be repeated (with the group trying different options in efforts to eliminate trickery) until everyone has got bored.

There's a lesson there somewhere ...

The secret is in the way you call your confederate, but no one will ever guess it. When you originally left the room with your newly appointed receiver you quickly explained that you would call them in one of three ways. If you say 'OK' it is the object on the left. If you say 'all right', it is the object in the middle. And if it is the object on the right, then you say 'ready'. The memory aid is the word 'oar'. The 'o' stands for 'OK' and is the letter and object on the left. The 'a' stands for 'all right' and is in the middle of the word. The 'r' stands for 'ready' and indicates the object on the right. As all these are natural words for you to use in asking someone to come back in, no one should suspect anything. Or rather, they will suspect everything, which comes to much the same thing. The real trick is not detected.

In this case, the significant information is part of the everyday background that we are inclined to filter out of perception. That in itself is a useful lesson.

Manipulating Minds Down on the Farm

The message of *Animal Farm*, easily decoded, is: workers good, capitalists bad, although the sheep helpfully put it instead as: 'Four legs good, two legs bad! Four legs good, two legs baaaaad!'

Things become more complicated however, when, over time, the pigs begin to dominate the farm, moving into the old farmer's house, eating

---

* These impressive techniques are adapted from Barry Robbin's book *Everybody's Book of Magic* (London and Letchworth: P.M. Productions Ltd, 2008).

at the farmer's table and even walking around on their hind legs! Not to forget, surreptitiously altering the founding principles that had been carefully painted on the side of the barn. Commandment Seven now reads: 'All animals are equal but some animals are more equal than others.' Seeing this, the sheep start bleating: 'Four legs good, two legs better! Four legs good, two legs beeeeetter!'

By the end of the book, when the animals peek through the window at the tyrannical pigs, now fully installed in the old farmhouse, dining and playing cards with the neighbouring human farmers, they now find it 'impossible to say which was which'. Orwell's final message is: workers good, capitalists and Communists are both equally bad.

The CIA liked the bleak view of Communism, of course, but they weren't so keen on Orwell's equation of Communists and capitalist exploitation. However, all it needed to 'press the right button', was that tiny tweak to the plot ...

Fast forward then to the CIA version of *1984*. In this, even as Winston and his lover, Julia, are gunned down, Winston defiantly shouts: 'Down with Big Brother!' Without wishing to be overly political, I think that we can agree that this sort of manipulation at least is very, very bad. But what about CIA *art*? Surprisingly perhaps, it is quite good – or at least innovative.

The theory was that since the Soviets favoured political commitment, realism, melody and representation, the 'anti-Communists' needed to favour discordant atonal music and Abstract Expressionism. Flying in the face of existing public taste, concerts and exhibitions of the most inaccessible, anti-populist, non-commercial avant garde artists flourished. The radicals were employed to do the bidding of the reactionaries.

After all, paradoxically, as one commentator put it, with the CIA dollar, you were free to be and do *anything* except, maybe, be critical of 'freedom'.

That only left intellectuals still thinking freely, not to say radically. There were people like Jean-Paul Sartre and Simone de Beauvoir, for instance, openly espousing the cause of radical politics in France. But then there was the special strategy to win over intellectuals – 'the battle for Picasso's mind,' as one former agent, Thomas Braden, put it in a television interview in the 1970s. Braden was responsible for dispensing money under the heading 'Congress for Cultural Freedom', but most of the people who he gave it out too, he noted, had no idea that the funds, and hence the 'artistic direction' actually came from the CIA. In time, intellectuals like the British philosopher Roger Scruton would spearhead the Agency's counter-revolutionary plans by travelling around Eastern Europe distributing *samizdat* copies of his lectures.

But the Agency's 'most important weapon of strategic (long-range) propaganda', as a former officer in the clandestine service described it, was neither journalism, nor trade unions, far less globe-trotting intellectuals. It was the humble book. Directly or indirectly, the CIA published or subsidised books on all topics, from African safaris and wildlife to translations of Machiavelli's *The Prince* into Swahili and the works of T.S. Eliot into Russian, to a competitor to Mao's little red book, entitled *Quotations from Chairman Liu*. It didn't matter to the Agency what the content was, as long as it served some subtle propaganda function. Nowadays the same strange manipulations take place behind the scenes of entities such as Google and Wikipedia on the Internet.

And although we have all read many times (so it must be at least partly true) that the CIA's primary mission during the Cold War was to fight Communism, the subversive sociolinguist philosopher, Noam Chomsky has pointed out that actually its priority has always been fighting democracy. From planting propaganda and corrupting elections to overthrowing democratic governments, from assassinating elected leaders to installing murderous dictators, the CIA has invariably opposed human rights and social justice and preferred instead dictatorships and the world-wide dominance of US-based corporations. Democracy doesn't come into it. In fact, democracy is rather a nuisance, along with concepts like 'truth', 'openness' and 'impartiality'.

It is for that reason that, as Chomsky puts it, the media is actually a mechanism for pervasive 'thought control' of the masses in the favour of an elite, and that before reading a newspaper, let alone looking at a TV programme, citizens need to 'undertake a course of intellectual self-defence to protect themselves from manipulation and control' (*Manufacturing Consent*, 1988).

Which, of course, is where this book came in ...

Appendix A: Three Lines Test

If some people are too quick to join a consensus, on the other hand, some people cling to ridiculous opinions based on faulty first impressions.

Take the columns in the diagram, for instance.

Arrange the three lines in order of size.

[Answer: B is the longest, A and C are equal.]

Curiously, because of the arrangement of the lines, some people will see line C as longer than line A. Some will even insist on it long after the illusion has been pointed out!

Mind Games: 31 Days To REDISCOVER Your Brain, Martin Cohen © 2010 John Wiley & Sons Inc

Sources and Suggestions for Further Reading

Week 1

Week one introduces the key themes of consciousness, symbols and the subconscious mind.

Days 1 and 2 Paul Broks raises this interesting question in his book *Into the Silent Land: Travels in Neuropsychology* (London: Atlantic, 2003), whereas (Day 2) the Reptile (Clotaire Rapaille) was speaking in a newspaper interview with the *South Florida Sun-Sentinel* on 25 March 2004, and since then has put his ideas into a book called *The Culture Code: An Ingenious Way to Understand Why People Around the World Buy and Live as They Do* (New York: Broadway Books, 2007). The discussion of rituals stretches into anthropology and classic social science works such as *The Elementary Forms of Religious Life* (1912) by Émile Durkheim. The 'classics' are often not as daunting as they sound for further reading, and are invariably available on the Internet, in a form suitable for a quick browse anyway.

Day 3 The mathematics of randomness is pursued in a fairly colourful way in *Randomness*, by D.J. Bennett (Cambridge, MA: Harvard University Press, 1999) – as well as in many other mathsy books.

Day 4 'Voices in the head' – a theme returned to at the end of the month (on Days 29 and 30) takes us well into psychology and so that classic work of Sigmund Freud's *On the Interpretation of Dreams* written back in 1900, might be dusted off here. The 1977 collection *Philosophical Essays on Dreaming*, edited by C.E.M. Dunlop (Ithaca, NY: Cornell University Press) is another useful reference work.

Day 5 'Favourite animals' is one of those children's games that seems to have come from somewhere, but no one (including me) is quite sure where exactly. However, it clearly continues the theme of the 'unconscious' and symbolism (especially sexual symbolism) and the scholarly source on that should be Freud, with books like *Totem and Taboo* (1913), in *The Standard Edition of the Complete Psychological Works of Sigmund Freud*, general editor James Straches, vol. 13 (London: The Hogarth Press, 1955).

Day 6 Looking at the causes of social trends, in this case the trend towards every-one being depressed and miserable, is the special interest of that under-rated philosopher, Émile Durkheim. His classic work *Suicide: A Study of Sociology* (1897) is interested in what causes people to become depressed, and that miser-able phenomenon, anomie, although that word itself seems to have been coined by another French philosopher, Jean-Marie Guyau.

Day 7 Our 'amateur monk' was describing her Trappist experience in an article in the newspaper, *Le Figaro* (7 July 2008). There are plenty of books on how to meditate in silence, and not much on the philosophy of it. But if you are content with just the former, *Door to Silence: An Anthology for Meditation*, by John Main (Norwich: Canterbury Press, 2006) is a good starter.

Week 2

Week 2 examines some of the 'practical research' by philosophers into how our minds work.

Days 8 and 9 Piaget describes his 'dotty experiments' in many works, but a good one to look at is *The Child's Conception of the World* (1929), trans. Joan and Andrew Tomlingson (London: Paladin, 1973). The, ah, 'revisionist' accounts of Piaget's sweeties come from one K. Wynn in 1992 ('Addition and subtraction by human infants', *Nature* 358, pp. 749–50), who used a series of changing arrangements behind a screen to distress the babies, while it was Stanislas Dehaene who thought to introduce Teddy into the mix (*The Number Sense: How the Mind Creates Mathematics*, Oxford: Oxford University Press, 1997). And the theory being applied, as mentioned in the Debriefing section, is that of behaviourism, set out in the 1925 book of the same name by its 'inventor', John Watson (London: Kegan Paul). Another key work by Jean Piaget is *The Language and Thought of the Child*, trans. M. and R. Gabain (London: Routledge, 2002).

Day 10 Dissonance is a concept from psychology and full details of the 'boring' experiment are in a paper by L. Festinger and J.M. Carlsmith, written in 1959, 'Cognitive consequences of forced compliance', *Journal of Abnormal and Social Psychology*, 58(2), 203–210.

Day 11 Oliver Sacks's book, *The Man Who Mistook His Wife for a Hat and Other Clinical Tales* (London: Duckworth,1985) cited in the text, is full of strange medical cases relating to how the memory does, or does not, function. A good reference guide to the history, the philosophy and the psychology of memory, with an interesting literary perspective, is D. Krell's *Of Memory: Reminiscence and Writing* (Bloomington: Indiana University Press, 1990).

Day 12 The investigation is about management and management is about individual aptitudes and skills – a notion that goes back to Plato's *Republic* where he talks of dividing up the philosophers from the rest of us – with the philosophers on top of course. There are many books on this presumably important topic, but I hesitate to recommend any of them. I haven't the necessary competencies, you see!

Marcus Buckingham and Curt Coffman, *First Break All the Rules: What the World's Greatest Managers Do Differently* (London: Simon and Schuster, 2001).

Day 13 Luck is not important to philosophers; it is, after all, irrational. However 'probability' and 'chance' are of great interest (after all they can be discussed using philosophy's otherwise rather pointless logical syntax) and again there are many references to both of these in classic accounts, such as David Hume's *A Treatise of Human Nature* (1739–40). But a good scholarly account of individual reactions to such questions of chance is the collection of papers edited by D. Kahneman, P. Slovic and A. Tversky, called *Judgement under Uncertainty: Heuristics and Biases* (Cambridge: Cambridge University Press, 1982). In the specific discussion of the 'Power of Partiality', I have benefited from Dorothy Coleman's interesting paper 'Partiality in Hume's moral theory' originally published in the *Journal of Value Inquiry* 26 (1992), pp. 95–104. See also Richard Wiseman, *The Luck Factor* (London: Arrow, 2004)

Day 14 Should I offer any help with self-help books? Or would to do so be a paradox? Certainly it would tend to turn this into a 'self-help book' after all. But for better or worse, such books are popular, and there is at least one respectable text: *Self-Help*, by Samuel Smiles, originally published in 1859 and now issued in the Oxford World's Classics series (Oxford: Oxford University Press, 2008). The aptly named Smiles has good news too: 'The spirit of self-help is the root of all genuine growth in the individual; and, exhibited in the lives of many, it constitutes the true source of national vigour and strength.'

Week 3

Week 3 goes a little more back to 'the world' to test if it is really quite how we imagined it.

Day 15 Professor Dennett's goggles are amongst several odd investigations in *Consciousness Explained* (Boston: Little, Brown, 1991). This book puts forward a 'multiple drafts' theory of mind, suggesting that there is no single central place no soul, no 'Cartesian theatre', where conscious experience occurs; instead there are 'various events of content-fixation occurring in various places at various times in the brain'. But other philosophers have objected that he misses the point entirely by simply redefining consciousness as 'an external property' and ignoring the all-important subjective aspect – being conscious'! Hence the book has been nicknamed in philosophy circles 'Consciousness Ignored'. Ho, ho, ho!

Day 16 Fire-walking and other nutty feats are the specialty of the contemporary physics teacher-cum-fire-walker, Dave Willey (day-job a physics professor at the

University of Pittsburgh) whose technical specifications I have borrowed here, as described in the *University Times* for the University of Pittsburgh.

Day 17 John Horton Conway writes about the mathematical rules behind complex behaviour in *On Numbers and Games* (London: Academic Press, 1976).

Day 18 The scratching nose phenomenon of proprioception is just one example of 'Mirror neurons and imitation learning as the driving force behind "the great leap forward" in human evolution' as V.S. Ramachandran put it in an influential essay of that title published by the web-journal, *Edge* (www.edge.org, 1 June 2000). Several cases of patients suffering from proprioception problems are also described by Oliver Sacks in *The Man Who Mistook His Wife for a Hat*. For the McGurk Effect, see *Nature* 264 (1976), pp. 746–748). You can cheat by seeing the effect on the web too, for example at YouTube.

Day 19 The coastal path is about fractal mathematics, and the way that complexity can arise from simple rules. And it also introduces the 'chaos' element of unpredictability. A good introduction to that topic is James Gleick's *Chaos: Making a New Science* (London: Vintage, 1988). See also Day 25.

Day 20 Being boring is a common phenomenon but there is only a rather limited interest in the topic in philosophy. Why might that be? At least that old Nazi, also known as an existentialist philosopher, Heidegger, apparently once gave a lecture which had about 100 pages on boredom, probably the most boring philosophical treatment ever of the subject! He focused on the tedium of waiting at train stations in particular.

Day 21 Apart from the ideas referenced in the main text, there is a substantial critique of the concept of 'normality' in sociology where it is argued that complicated hierarchies of 'norms' dictate our everyday lives. See, for example, Durkheim, again, this time the *Rules of Sociological Method* (1895).

Week 4

We finish the month with not so much some light reading as some very heavy reading. That's what happens when you wake up your brain!

Day 22 Molyneux's problem appears in *An Essay Concerning Human Understanding*, Book 2, chapter 9, by John Locke. 'Mary's Room' appears in Frank Jackson's article 'Epiphenomenal qualia', *Philosophical Quarterly*, 32 (1982), 127–136 and was extended in the book *What Mary Didn't Know* (1986), notes from *Journal of Philosophy*, 83 (1986), 291–295. Then there's Peter Ludlow, Yujin Nagasawa and Daniel Stoljar, eds, *There's Something about Mary: Essays on Phenomenal Consciousness and Frank Jackson's Knowledge Argument* (Cambridge, MA: MIT Press, 2004).

Day 23 The way the mind creates order out of chaos is a central theme of both psychology and philosophy. A dry general account is David Byrne's *Complexity*

Theory and the Social Sciences (London: Routledge, 1998) and a livelier one is *Deep Simplicity: Chaos, Complexity and the Emergence of Life* by John Gribbin (London: Allen Lane, 2004).See also Day 19.

Day 24 Cascade theory. The classic text here is Charles Mackay's *Memoirs of Extraordinary Popular Delusions and the Madness of Crowds* (London: R. Bentley, 1841). The fattening measurements of the 'fat is bad' movement are described in a 2007 book *Good Calories, Bad Calories,* by Gary Taubes (not pronounced 'Tubby') (New York: Alfred A. Knopf, 2007). Ancel Keys's articles are 'Atherosclerosis: a problem in newer public health', *Journal of Mount Sinai Hospital NY* 20 (1953), pp. 118–139 and 'Coronary heart disease in seven countries', *Circulation* 41 (1970) (suppl. 1), pp. 1–211. See also the Surgeon General's Report on Nutrition and Health (1988). Page 103, for example, talks of 'causal agents' for disease 'such as smoking or a high saturated fat intake'. Table 4–1 (p. 180) lists 'cancer deaths attributed to various factors' squarely putting 'diet' as the main culprit, with tobacco only coming in second. The full report is at http://profiles.nlm.nih.gov/NN/B/C/Q/G/

Day 25 Chaos theory and the workings of the market are explained at rather excessive length in the undeservedly popular (but I'll cite it anyway) book, *The Black Swan: The Impact of the Highly Improbable* (London: Allen Lane, 2007) by Nassim Nicholas Taleb (see also Day 19). I made a similar point eight years earlier in my extremely relevant and well worth recommending *101 Philosophy Problems* (London, Routledge, 1999), citing, yes, black swans – but no one respects 'philosophy' books – they want ones by economists and mathematicians instead. And so to John von Neumann, 'Method in the Physical Sciences', in *The Unity of Knowledge,* edited by L. Leary (1955), reprinted in John von Neumann, *The Neumann Compendium,* ed. F. Bródy and Tibor Vámos (Singapore, World Scientific, 1995), p. 628.

Day 26 All those tactics! But the original and classic account is very short and to the point: Schopenhauer's mini-book *The Art of Always Being Right* published back in 1831 (introduced by A.C. Grayling, London: Gibson Square, 2004). Francis Wheen's book is, *How Mumbo-Jumbo Conquered the World: A Short History of Modern Delusions* (London: Fourth Estate, 2004).

Day 27 Subliminal messages became a great scare in the 1950s, a time when books like Vance Packard's *The Hidden Persuaders* (New York: Pocket Books, 1957) and John Kenneth Galbraith's book, *The Affluent Society,* (in full, *In Praise of the Consumer Critic: Economics and The Affluent Society Consumption in Mainstream Economics,* Boston: Houghton Mifflin) a year later were all the rage. But the general message of how 'consumers' are led by 'producers' (businesses and advertisers) is even more relevant today; see Wilson B. Key, *Subliminal Seduction: Ad Media's Manipulation of a Not So Innocent America* (New York: Signet, 1973). The Beatles' song, 'Lucy in the Sky with Diamonds' is often said to have been a reference to LSD (geddit?) and indeed the lyrics seem to portray a druggy day out. However, the Beatles always denied this was the case. John Lennon, who wrote the larger part of the song, insisted it was about a picture his son Julian painted while in kindergarten. When his proud Dad asked what the picture was of, Julian said it was his friend, Lucy, in the sky, with diamonds. (As reported by the BBC here: http://news.bbc.co.uk/2/hi/8278785.stm)

In 1990 the band Judas Priest was involved in a civil action that alleged they were responsible for the self-inflicted gunshot wounds of two youths in Reno, Nevada, USA. During the trial it was alleged that as well as general incantations to 'do it', parts of the band's songs, if played backwards, said things like 'I took my life'. A soundclip of this, relevant to both Day 18 and Day 20, is at http://www.reversespeech.com/judas.htm

Day 28 Psychological Perspectives on Prayer, by Leslie John Francis and Jeff Astley (Leominster: Gracewing, 2001) catalogues numerous examples of plants that were given regular prayers coming out ahead of unloved ones. See also Franklin Loehr, *The Power of Prayer on Plants* (Garden City, NY: Doubleday, 1959).

Day 29 Hildegard's visions are discussed in Sabina Flanagan's *Hildegard of Bingen 1088–1179: A Visionary Life* (London: Routledge, 1998) and Jung ponders his own fears in his partially autobiographical book *Memories, Dreams, Reflections* (1956), recorded and edited by Aniela Jaffé; translated from the German by Richard and Clara Winston. (London: Fontana, 1995).

Day 31 The best introduction to this sort of sinister mind control remains Orwell's two classic novels, *Animal Farm* (1946), and *1984* which was written long before that date – in 1949. But make sure you get the untampered-with versions!

Index

Also by Martin Cohen

Philosophical Tales:
Being an Alternative History
Revealing the Characters,
the Plots, and the Hidden Scenes
that make up the True Story
of Philosophy

ISBN: 978-1-4051-4037-9 | Paperback | 296 pages | 2008

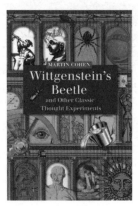

Wittgenstein's Beetle
and Other Classic Thought
Experiments

ISBN: 978-1-4051-2192-7 | Paperback | 142 pages | 2004

For information and to order please visit
www.wiley.com/go/philosophy